Routledge Revivals

The Indian Earthquake

First published in 1935, this book provides a comprehensive overview of the 1934 Nepal-Bihar earthquake, giving a background to the earthquake zone, describing the event itself and surveying the ensuing devastation. The author also looks at the government's actions and the response of India's other states as well as the religious and social dimension to the reaction — exemplified by Mahatma Gandhi. The book examines how the earthquake was compounded by a severe flood that occurred shortly before, how preparations for the monsoon season were made in an attempt to limit further destruction and the subsequent recommendations for more earthquake resistant urban planning.

The Indian Earthquake

C.F. Andrews

First published in 1935
by George Allen & Unwin

This edition first published in 2016 by Routledge
2 Park Square, Milton Park, Abingdon, Oxon, OX14 4RN
and by Routledge
711 Third Avenue, New York, NY 10017

Routledge is an imprint of the Taylor & Francis Group, an informa business

© 1935 C.F. Andrews

All rights reserved. No part of this book may be reprinted or reproduced
or utilised in any form or by any electronic, mechanical, or other means,
now known or hereafter invented, including photocopying and recording,
or in any information storage or retrieval system, without permission in
writing from the publishers.

Publisher's Note
The publisher has gone to great lengths to ensure the quality of this
reprint but points out that some imperfections in the original copies may
be apparent.

Disclaimer
The publisher has made every effort to trace copyright holders and
welcomes correspondence from those they have been unable to contact.

A Library of Congress record exists under LC control number: 41013762

ISBN 13: 978-1-138-21185-8 (hbk)
ISBN 13: 978-1-315-45161-9 (ebk)
ISBN 13: 978-1-138-21192-6 (pbk)

Printed in the United Kingdom
by Henry Ling Limited

The
INDIAN EARTHQUAKE

by
C. F. ANDREWS

LONDON
GEORGE ALLEN & UNWIN LTD
MUSEUM STREET

FIRST PUBLISHED IN 1935

All rights reserved

PRINTED IN GREAT BRITAIN BY
UNWIN BROTHERS LTD., WOKING

DEDICATED
TO MY FRIEND
RAJENDRA PRASAD
WITH DEEP AFFECTION

"Out of the great tragedy that has overwhelmed us, we earnestly hope that some good may permanently endure in the shape of a united Nation, joined together in common sorrow and common effort to overcome it, having faith in one another."

STATEMENT BY THE
CENTRAL RELIEF COMMITTEE

February 3, 1934

INTRODUCTORY NOTE

THE profits derived from the sale of this book will be given to the relief of those who have suffered from the great earthquake and from the floods which followed during the monsoon. The manuscript has been held over in order to include, while I was on the spot in India, an account of the damage wrought by the floods, which has been hardly less serious than that already done by the earthquake itself.

In writing about the earthquake I have used freely material published in India, both in the different reports of the Central Relief Committee and also in the *Statesman Earthquake Report*. I would gratefully acknowledge my debt to these, and also to a lecture delivered by Sir Edward Pascoe, on "The Indian Earthquake," before the Royal Society of Arts.

The manuscript, which I had prepared before reaching India, has been revised by my friend, Rajendra Prasad, Chairman of the Relief Committee, while I have stayed with him at Patna and Wardha. Other friends in India have helped me in a similar manner.

May I express a hope that this book will find its way into public libraries where the poor may read it, who cannot afford to buy copies of their own, and that it may also be read, through translations, in European countries which have a deep sympathy with the East? The village people in India, who suffered, are the poorest in the world; and the poor in other countries will be able to understand and feel their sufferings most keenly.

Any help for the sufferers should be sent direct to the Treasurer, Earthquake Central Relief Fund, Patna, India.

C. F. ANDREWS

PATNA, *1934*

CONTENTS

CHAPTER		PAGE
	Introductory Note by the Author	11
I.	The Scene Described	15
II.	The Earthquake Zone	26
III.	The Devastated Area	32
IV.	What Science Tells Us	40
V.	The Floods in Orissa	48
VI.	The All-India Response	53
VII.	How Government Acted	60
VIII.	The Moral Problem	68
IX.	Mahatma Gandhi in Bihar	78
X.	The Great Experiment	93
XI.	The Spirit of Service	103
XII.	The Monsoon Floods	111
XIII.	International Help	118
	Appendix : A Letter from Pierre Cérésole	123

THE INDIAN EARTHQUAKE

CHAPTER I

THE SCENE DESCRIBED

i

THE principal earthquake shock, which did such damage to the land in North Bihar and destroyed thousands of human lives, occurred at 2.15 p.m. on January 15, 1934.

Preliminary tremors had already warned people of the imminent danger before the fatal shock came. There was everywhere an immediate rush into the open. Only where, in the towns, the streets were narrow was the number of deaths large. While thousands perished (for the worst shocks covered more than fifteen thousand square miles), there were many marvellous escapes.

It is hardly possible to describe in writing the horrors of those few moments for all those who were in the earthquake zone itself. The solid ground was rocking to and fro beneath their feet, and the earth opened in great cracks on every side. In less than three minutes whole towns were reduced to ruins, and millions of villagers in panic believed that the end of the world had come.

If we who are called upon to sympathize with the sufferers are to do so with intelligence, it is necessary to get a clear mental picture of what the scene was like.

THE INDIAN EARTHQUAKE

One such account, vividly related, is given us by an eye-witness in Monghyr, who has described what happened in a pamphlet called *Devastated Bihar*.

The day, he states, was bitterly cold, and it had been preceded by a strangely chilling spell of unsettled weather as though the mountain atmosphere to the north had been disturbed. A strong west wind swept across the open plain at the foot of the Himalayas, making the cold still more intense.

Hindus had gathered in many thousands, in spite of the inclement weather, in order to bathe in the River Ganges. For January 15th was a Hindu religious festival, when bathing was auspicious. At Monghyr, which is on the banks of the Ganges, a very large crowd had collected. The ceremonial bath in the Ganges had been taken. Men and women were in the bazaar purchasing small things for their children before returning home.

With the Muslims also the day was a semi-festive occasion. The great Muslim 'Id (festival) was to be held on the next day, and many had come in to Monghyr to complete their shopping before it began. Others were lying down enjoying their siesta when the earthquake occurred.

Precisely at 2.15 p.m. a rumbling began in the air, and many looked up to the sky thinking that an aeroplane was overhead. But at the same moment the earth began to tremble violently beneath their feet. Fortunately the greatest shock did not come all at once. People realized what was happening, and a stampede was made to reach the open space outside the tottering buildings. But in the

THE SCENE DESCRIBED

congested part of the bazaar there was hardly any wide area left in which to find an escape.

The shock increased in intensity every second, as the solid earth swayed to and fro. Soon it became quite impossible to keep one's balance, and most people were thrown down. Houses swung from east to west, and walls began to crack in all directions. Even then, however, some of the buildings seemed able to withstand the shock.

But the rumbling suddenly deepened into a roar, and it seemed as though a thousand aeroplanes were sounding overhead. At the climax came a stunning noise, like great guns in a battle zone, and the death-knell of Monghyr was sounded. The town collapsed in ruin. There must have been sixty thousand people involved in the awful disaster in Monghyr alone, and the marvel is that out of that number so many escaped alive.

The deafening noise and the crash of falling buildings were succeeded at once by a darkness that could almost be felt. It was caused by the thick masses of dust, which blotted out the light of the sun and made the air almost unbreathable. It filled the lungs and caused a choking which verged on suffocation.

Then, after a few moments, a glimmer of light reappeared, and it was possible through the haze to see the town in a state of collapse, with walls still tottering to their fall, one upon another, like a pack of cards. To render any immediate help was impossible. The open ground was still shaking, and cracks were appearing in all directions. Shrieks from the maimed and dying were mingled with the roar of the earthquake and the crash of

THE INDIAN EARTHQUAKE

ruined masonry. In some instances men's hair turned grey during that awful moment of fear. To be alive was almost a greater horror than to be killed by the shock.

ii

The terror that followed the havoc wrought by the earthquake was more heart-rending still. Men and women were seen throwing up their hands in hysterical dread, as if they had gone mad. As soon as the survivors had recovered their senses and could stand upright, they hurried to search for those dearest to them who lay beneath the ruins. Frantic haste was uppermost in everybody's mind, as the cries for help grew more and more piercing. Tearing away the *débris* with their bare hands, they sought desperately to rescue children and women from beneath the heap of ruins.

One last horror was fortunately absent. In spite of all the inflammable material of the bazaar, no conflagration ensued. Thus the tragedy of Tokyo and Yokohama was not repeated in Bihar. But the agony was hardly less intense. For the long-drawn wail of wounded men and women and little children rent the sky.

Those who survived have tried to tell us the dreadful effect of that cry upon them. At first it was paralysing to hear. Then it drove them almost mad in their desperate efforts to tear away the masonry from broken limbs. They raced against time to rescue those who were lying half-dead beneath the ruins.

Evening came very rapidly on that January afternoon. The night that followed is harder to picture even than

THE SCENE DESCRIBED

the day which had preceded. No lights were anywhere available, and the sky was still obscure with the dust-clouds filling the air. The icy wind swept down from the Himalayas, and there was scarcely any protection or shelter. Further shocks throughout the night added to the general alarm. The moans of the dying sounded piteously all through the dark hours. There were those who were hopelessly crushed, with solid masonry pinning them down. They pleaded to be put out of their pain.

That night of dread was but the beginning of long days and longer nights of misery. Few were able to get normal sleep, because slight shocks continued. At Monghyr itself relief was hurried forward as fast as possible, for it was on the banks of the Ganges and near a railway, which was still in working order. But remote towns, such as Sitamarhi and Motihari, could not be reached on account of the fissures in the roads and broken railway and road bridges. To some sufferers in remote regions the first relief came from aeroplanes flying low. But these were often unable to find a level spot to land and take off again while they carried on their work of first-aid.

iii

A story is told by one of the survivors concerning an almost unbelievable scene that he witnessed in the bed of the River Ganges itself, not far from Monghyr. To those who have not realized fully the extent of the disaster, this incident would seem on the face of it impossible; and yet it comes from a well-authenticated source.

THE INDIAN EARTHQUAKE

The writer states that he was standing, in the open, on the banks of the River Ganges when the first earthquake shock began and the ground swayed beneath his feet. He was looking towards the river, whose waters were low at that season of the year. There was an island in the middle of the stream. On the side nearest to himself the waters were shallow and people were bathing. On the further side the river was deeper and a small steamer along with some country boats was plying to and fro, ferrying people across. For a moment he saw the bed of the Ganges upheaved so that the water on either side of the island disappeared and land rose where water had been before. The steamer and country boats swayed to and fro as they were lifted up by the upheaval and stranded. Then as suddenly the land sank back and the water of the Ganges rushed on. All the boats were upset, and he could see people struggling in the flood. One who was at his side, a Muslim, cried out *Quyāmat* (Judgment!), thinking that the Day of Judgment had come.

Another story has reached me in a personal letter from Sir Tej Bahadur Sapru of Allahabad. A little child had wandered in a bewildered manner into his compound, long after the earthquake, dazed and famished and half-dead. The boy was very kindly treated by the household, and when he came to himself he explained how he had seen his own village disappear, swallowed up by a huge rent in the earth, his family all perishing in the overthrow. He was so dazed that he hardly knew after that what had occurred, until he was rescued by my

THE SCENE DESCRIBED

friend in Allahabad. He informed them that his own village had been near Sitamarhi in North Bihar—a place which was over two hundred miles distant.

Cases of aberration, both mental and physical, such as this have not been uncommon. Children who have lost both their parents have been picked up by kind-hearted people hundreds of miles away from the scene of the great disaster.

Another eye-witness wrote as follows: "At Suki we saw some strange and almost unbelievable sights. Along the banks of the Noom River there have been big open fissures everywhere, and houses have suffered immense damage. At one point we saw a house split into two, one part of it standing on land which had subsided by about seven or eight feet, the other part standing on land which had not subsided to the same extent, the two parts looking as if they were two houses built on different levels in the way they build in the Hills. A barn for storing straw had been shifted some fifteen to twenty feet along with the land on which it stood; and we were shown a palm-tree which had been removed in a similar manner.

"What we saw here reminded us of what we had seen at Motihari along the bank of the small lake. We were told that one plot of land was moving, during the earthquake, with a cow standing on it. The cow was rescued after the catastrophe, trembling but unhurt.

"The river is, of course, choked. All these things appear to indicate that large blocks of land, to great depths, have been bodily shifted."

THE INDIAN EARTHQUAKE

In the *Statesman Earthquake Report* there is the photograph of a tree, still erect, whose solid trunk has been split in two by a fissure running along the ground. The tree appears to be still alive, with this big gap in the ground beneath it and its whole stem split asunder.

The account of another incident reached me in a letter from a missionary lady, who had hurried to Monghyr from a neighbouring town soon after the earthquake had occurred. Already, she wrote, the work of rescue and recovery of the dead had begun. She stood with others on the only solid piece of masonry, which was still unbroken, and watched the rescue work. The men cleared away the rubble just beneath where she was standing, and one body after another was brought out and laid on the ground outside. Seven were taken from beneath that one piece of ruin, and all were dead. The tragedy was so great that she could not bear the sight of it.

Even as late as a month after the great shock deaths still occurred owing to buildings already shaken suddenly crumbling into ruin.

Marvellous escapes were also recorded. The Metropolitan of India, Bishop Foss Westcott of Calcutta, had only just time to rush out into the open, from the verandah of the bungalow where he was staying, when the walls collapsed, leaving behind only a heap of bricks and rubble.

As the facts slowly came to light, the miracle, which was on everyone's lips, was the smallness of the death-roll, when compared with the magnitude of the disaster. It was pointed out that if the shock had occurred in the

THE SCENE DESCRIBED

middle of the night the casualties might have been many times greater. For in the cold weather in North Bihar it is the custom to shut both doors and windows at night. Everyone would have been indoors and surrounded by darkness. Escape, in that case, would have been very difficult, and deaths in the villages as well as in the towns would have been much more numerous.

As it was, the men in the villages were out of doors, and most of the women and children were also in the open. The household work had been finished; there was no duty at that time which kept the women inside the home.

iv

When the full reports came in it was found that only in the narrow, congested streets of the large towns in North Bihar was the death-roll very high. In these quarters, as we have seen, there was no open space where the townspeople could escape.

It is noticeable that the number of Europeans killed was exceedingly small. This was because they were living in houses with open spaces round them, and there was ample time to run out of doors. One tragic incident was the death of Miss Francis Christian at Monghyr, who had escaped with safety into the open, and then remembered her dog. She ran back to fetch it, and was crushed to death beneath the ruins of the house.

A letter was read before the Royal Society of Arts by Mr. Scarth, which he had received from his daughter.

THE INDIAN EARTHQUAKE

"I hope," she wrote, "I shall never go through such a ghastly experience again. It was raining, and we were within the house, scattered about, when the earthquake came.

"There was a long warning, thank God! and we had just time to get hold of the boys and rush into the garden before the worst of it began. We watched the house shaking like a jelly for about three minutes. The chimneys came crashing down. We were in a panic, for Michael could not be found!

"The bearer, who was with him, had rushed with him to the other side of the house. The earthquake still continued, and I do not know how long it lasted. The house was still standing when it was over, but it was *quite* uninhabitable."

V

The number of those who were killed by the earthquake is variously given by different authorities.

The Government figures, which are the minimum and register only the deaths accounted for and recorded, amount to 7,252 for the Bihar area, and approximately 3,400 for the Nepal Valley. Those who know the extreme difficulty of reckoning exact figures in a disaster of this kind would probably add largely to the Government's official total, in order to make up for those whose bodies have never been found. Under the ruins and within the huge crevices there are likely to be very many dead who have never been counted at all.

THE INDIAN EARTHQUAKE

Rajendra Prasad[1] cabled to me in London that the number of dead could hardly be less than twenty thousand. Most of the estimates made by the Indian workers, in different earthquake local areas, are higher than those given by Government officers.

Yet even if we make full allowance for the larger number suggested, the fact stands out that the death-roll was small compared with the intensity of the shock and the largeness of the population included in the earthquake zone.

[1] The Indian leader of Bihar. As far as possible, I have avoided giving Indian titles in a book intended mainly for Western readers. Only when a title is very familiar (such as "Mahatma Gandhi") have I used it.

CHAPTER II

THE EARTHQUAKE ZONE

i

NORTH BIHAR, where the earthquake wrought such havoc, lies within a narrow belt at the foot of the Himalaya Mountains, which has long been recognized by geologists as a "danger zone."

Two very severe earthquakes, one in Assam in 1897 and the other in the Punjab in 1905, have occurred within this belt during the last forty years.

In addition to these, seven other shocks of considerable intensity have happened in still more recent times. The worst of these was at Pegu in Burma in May 1930. Though this was beyond the Himalaya boundary, it belonged to the same series of shocks.

ii

I can vividly remember the earthquake in the North Punjab in 1905, called the Kangra Valley Earthquake, for I was living in the heart of the old city of Delhi at the time, in an ancient building, which felt the shock at its maximum intensity. The one thing that remains in my mind, after all these years, is the sound of the terrified screaming of hundreds of birds on the trees outside. The fear expressed in those screams haunted me for many days afterwards.

At the time we imagined we were at the centre of the

THE EARTHQUAKE ZONE

shock, but later on we found out that this was in the Kangra Valley, more than two hundred miles distant. In the same way the people in Calcutta, during the recent earthquake, imagined that they were in the intensive earthquake area, while in reality they were hundreds of miles away.

iii

One of the chief causes of the delay in sending news out to the whole world concerning the tragedy of North Bihar was the isolation that immediately took place. All the telegraph lines were broken down. Railway communication had been cut off. The River Ganges itself is difficult to cross at this part of its course. Patna, the capital of Bihar, is on the south of the river, while the chief destruction was on the north. Bridges were destroyed in all directions on the north of the Ganges, and even the roads were torn up by the convulsion that had taken place. Only aeroplanes, at first, were able to overcome these obstructions.

iv

Sir James Sifton, the Governor, was one of the first to fly in an aeroplane over the devastated area. He wrote in his appeal as follows:

"In the towns of North Bihar there is probably not one masonry house which is altogether undamaged, while thousands of houses are completely destroyed, with not a wall standing. In one congested bazaar of Monghyr the ruin was so complete that for days it was not possible

THE INDIAN EARTHQUAKE

to see where the line of the street had been amid the acres of destroyed houses. The urban population affected is not less than half a million souls, some of the towns which have been wrecked having a population of from fifty to sixty thousand inhabitants.

"The people of these towns are now for the most part camping in open spaces, close to the towns, in grass and bamboo sheds and other makeshifts. They must continue to do so for months to come, till money and material are made available for them to rebuild their homes.

"Those townspeople who are in the greatest distress are the small shopkeepers and people of the professional classes. The richer people have some reserves to fall back on. Artisans and labourers will have work in plenty at remunerative rates. But a large majority of the middle-class people, who have escaped with little but their lives, must have substantial help to rebuild their homes and start life again.

"In the villages the destruction of houses was not very severe. Mud-built huts have survived where masonry collapsed, and the disaster to the agriculturist has taken a different form. Soldiers who have flown over Bihar liken it to a battlefield in the destruction of the land which has taken place. Over a large area the cultivators have had their lands spoiled by fountains of water, which poured out from fissures and gushers and spread sand over the fields to a depth varying from a few inches to three feet, or even more. The full extent of this damage will not be known for a long time.

THE EARTHQUAKE ZONE

"There is a further danger, which at this time is not calculable. It is known that the earthquake in many places has changed the level of the country. Embanked roads are found now to be reduced to the level of the surrounding country. Old waterways are not functioning, and streams have changed their course. Where land is still in a deltaic condition, as it is in North Bihar, even a slight change of levels completely alters the drainage, and it becomes almost certain that the next monsoon will cause severe inundation over tracts of land that were formerly immune from flood.[1]

"The section of the community that has suffered very severely, outside the towns, includes sugar-cane growers. The factories, with their bungalows, are destroyed; and a growing crop of half a milllion tons of sugar-cane has to be written off as loss.

"Reconstruction cannot be effected in a period of weeks or months, but will extend over years."

iv

Dr. Fermor, the geological expert, has given us some interesting statistics, showing the intensity and distance of propagation of the shock that wrought such damage in North Bihar.[2] He points out that this earthquake was distinctly felt up to a distance of one thousand miles. Thus the complete area of the shock, if the distance had been the same in all directions, would have been 3,150,000 square miles. This makes the Bihar earthquake, in its

[1] This forecast has proved true. See Chapter XII.
[2] *Statesman Earthquake Record*, p. 19.

THE INDIAN EARTHQUAKE

area of shock transmission, one of the greatest ever recorded. The most extensive field of "felt" shock from an earthquake, before this, was in the Charleston disaster of 1886, which covered about 2,800,000 square miles. The Assam Earthquake of 1897 was "felt" over 1,750,000 square miles, and that in the Kangra Valley in 1905 over 2,000,000 square miles.

With regard to intensity, the rate of its acceleration through the earth's surface was probably 10 to 11 feet per second; but the exact rate has not yet been finally determined. In the Assam and Kangra Valley earthquakes the rate of 13 to 14 feet per second was registered. In the Pegu Earthquake of 1930 the rate was 4 to 7 feet per second.

Apart from the recent Indian earthquake, by far the most disastrous within living memory was that which happened at Tokyo and Yokohama in Japan in the year 1923. While the area of maximum intensity in Bihar was far in excess of that in Japan, the destruction of human life in Japan was more than ten times as great as that in Bihar.

Two reasons accounted for this:

(1) The centre of the Japanese earthquake included the two cities of Tokyo and Yokohama, which together contained an urban population of nearly three million souls.

(2) A raging fire, starting in the middle of Tokyo, burnt down a great part of the city and completed the havoc.

Thus the death-roll mounted up, in the course of a

THE EARTHQUAKE ZONE

few days, to hundreds of thousands, and one horror was added to another. The whole world stood aghast at a tragedy so immense, and every country came to the aid of Japan in her heroic work of reconstruction. More than two million pounds sterling was subscribed from outside.

The work of reconstruction in Tokyo and Yokohama has taken more than ten years to complete, and a sum of over fifty million pounds sterling has been spent in this great act of national recovery.

It was inevitable that the imagination of mankind should be more deeply impressed by the Tokyo disaster than by that in North Bihar. For the whole setting was far more tragically sudden and dramatic. The panorama of the metropolis of the great Japanese Empire being burnt to the ground was filmed and reproduced all over the world, and a deep impression was left on millions of people's minds.

No picture of misery so immediately arresting could be recorded in India, though the illustrations which appeared on the screens showed the extent of the tragedy far more clearly than the meagre newspaper reports. In the long run, however, as each expert adviser relates, the ruin wrought in North Bihar is hardly less serious than that which happened in Japan.

CHAPTER III

THE DEVASTATED AREA

i

THE strange form which the Bihar earthquake has taken has expressed itself in the very soil itself, whereon the villagers depend for their daily bread. Not only has the earth been upheaved for miles in some directions and cracked in others, but large regions have been rendered practically useless for cultivation owing to the eruption from below the ground of immense volumes of sand.

Volcanoes pour out streams of lava which enrich the soil; but the reverse has happened in North Bihar. Through innumerable small craters there has been spread over the earth, not fertilizing lava, but fine glistening sand.

In some places where the layer of sand is thin it may be possible to remove it or to plough it in with tractors. But in other parts there seems very little hope of any human effort being effective. Therefore some of this area may pass entirely out of cultivation and become barren.

This, however, is not the only danger that has threatened the village cultivator, for the levels of the whole country have been disturbed by this tremendous upheaval, and the natural drainage of the soil has been upset. The flood-water, which helped the paddy cultivation in ordinary years, has remained much longer on the

THE DEVASTATED AREA

ground during the recent season owing to the obstructions caused by the earthquake. Through the injury done by this excess of water, much of the paddy crop has been destroyed, and the villagers have suffered grievous loss. All this will be fully explained later.[1]

ii

It is easy for anyone who passes through the villages to see how very fertile the land is in North Bihar. The soil has been formed by layers of mud and silt washed down from the high mountains. It receives abundance of rain and sunshine.

But while the land is fertile the dwellers on it, in their overcrowded villages, remain poverty-stricken. This is not the place to go fully into all the economic causes of this poverty. But now that the fabric of society has been violently torn asunder by the earthquake, the work of reconstruction should include the planning out of a better social order, side by side with new town and village planning.

Not only will the whole system of land tenure need to be overhauled, but also the evils of child-marriage and untouchability, which tend to create an enfeebled and prolific population, must be boldly faced and overcome.

One of those who went in an aeroplane to the scene of the disaster was the Lord Mayor of Calcutta, Mr. S. K. Basu. In his appeal to his fellow-citizens he made a significant statement, that the entire structure of civilized

[1] See Chapter XII.

society in the earthquake area would have to be built up again from its foundation—the ruin has been so complete.

He stated that in the chief towns, which were fairly prosperous before, not one house had been left undamaged. The majority of them had been injured beyond repair. The drainage system had also been choked. The water supply had been thrown out of gear, and the majority of wells had been ruined. All public buildings had suffered.

Wherever the Mayor looked out from the aeroplane, as he circled over the scene of desolation, he found the earth cut up into gaping fissures, which ran for miles and miles. Their track could easily be marked out by the naked eye right across the country.

"Whatever," he relates, "came in the way of these all-devouring chasms was swallowed up. Masonry, buildings, trees, roads, railways even, were engulfed. In some instances men and cattle disappeared one moment, and then were thrown out again at the next moment by the uprush of subsoil water, opening up the surface with immense force."

He describes how, flying very low in a de Haviland Moth plane, he had full opportunity of observing the devastation that had been wrought. He found the whole country spotted with countless little mounds of sand, about one foot or more above the ground, removed from one another at a distance of 5 to 10 feet.

These formed the craters of small geysers, or gushers, through which the subsoil water had forced itself up and

THE DEVASTATED AREA

spread over the country. As he saw the whole panorama, with these numberless pit-holes still throwing up sand, it seemed to him like some witch's cauldron bubbling over.

"The aftermath," he continues, "of this awful dance of Nature has taken the form of extensive deposits of sand, covering the finest agricultural land of the province. Can the poor cultivator, with no reserve of ordinary subsistence, find even his humblest food and raiment for two or three years, if at all he can be set on his legs again?"

iii

A newspaper correspondent, who also flew over North Bihar, has computed that the lives of every one of the twelve million people included in the earthquake area have been deranged and thrown out of gear by what has happened, and that it will be many months before any return to normal existence can be expected.

"Probably," he writes, "the most impressive feature of the disaster is not the smashed towns, but the astounding large-scale alterations to the whole structure of the countryside. Over thousands of square miles the land is traversed by enormous jagged fissures, and filled with objects which, from the air, look like small volcanic craters. Out of these, circles of sand or grey mud have spread over the fields. The road and railway bridges are down in all directions. Hundreds of miles of railway lines have become wrecked, metals having been, in some places, thrown clean off the track.

"At one place I noticed an abandoned train standing

THE INDIAN EARTHQUAKE

in a station, the whole length of which was traversed by an enormous crack, several feet wide. Since the entire devastated area consists of flat alluvial land, large blocks of which have suffered vertical displacement of several inches, if not feet, and have in several places already changed the courses of streams, it seems certain that there will be extensive alterations in the drainage of the country when the next monsoon rains come down, resulting in disastrous flooding."

This prediction has already been fulfilled.

iv

One of the most serious consequences of the earthquake, which at once engaged the attention of the relief workers, has been the choking up with sand of almost all the wells in the area that is worst affected. There has also been serious damage done to the masonry of the larger wells that are in most frequent use. The villagers and the townspeople have hitherto depended on these for their supply of drinking water, but now the water has been fouled and become undrinkable. No problem was more urgent than this in the first days of the recovery, after the earthquake shocks had died down.

v

Since a hope has been expressed by those who have encouraged me to write this book, that it may be widely read in Europe and America, it may be well to give some idea of the extent of the earthquake in terms of area and population in the West.

THE DEVASTATED AREA

It has been computed, for instance, that the area of maximum intensity would correspond in England to a rectangle within the four points of London, Stamford, Crewe, and Malvern. In America it would represent an area almost as large as the State of Connecticut. If the shock had taken place in either of these areas it is likely that every house made of brick or stone would have been damaged. Furthermore, in spite of the Bihar population being rural, it is so dense that even these densely populated areas hardly carry a greater number of people, if we exclude from the former rectangle the city of London itself. For the density of population in North Bihar runs up to eight hundred persons to the square mile.

Several whole countries in Europe, such as Holland, Switzerland, or Denmark, might be compared with the intensive earthquake zone. One calculation has been set forward making this area of maximum shock as big as the whole of Scotland, and including more than four times its population.

When we turn to the larger circle of earth-shaking, wherein much damage was done but very few lives were lost, we find that this would represent in Europe a space contained within the four points of London, Riga, Belgrade, and Marseilles, and in America within the area circumscribed by Boston, Ottawa, Cleveland, and Washington.

Even places that were six hundred miles distant—as far as Milan is from London, or Charleston from Philadelphia—the shock was so severe that people ran

THE INDIAN EARTHQUAKE

out of their houses in fear, and damage to property occurred.[1]

vi

One geographical factor, to which attention has already been called, will make all future relief work on a large scale extremely difficult.

North Bihar is isolated on its southern border from the rest of India by the shifting river-bed of the Ganges, which for a distance of over two hundred miles cannot be spanned by any bridge. Even ferrying on a steam ferry presents difficulties, and takes up a great deal of valuable time. For instance, a journey from Patna on the south to Muzaffarpur on the north bank, which is only thirty-five miles away as the crow flies, can hardly be accomplished in under four hours. The use of an aeroplane to visit the area has its limitations because in this thickly cultivated rice-growing country, where every foot of land is valuable, large open spaces for landing hardly exist.

Just as this difficulty of access accounted for the slowness of the news coming through, so it has already made the transport of building material on a large scale a laborious process. Both men and materials have to be brought to the scene of action at a great cost of time and labour.

In Nepal State, which formed the second intensive earthquake zone, the difficulties are greater still. The railhead, a few miles beyond Raxaul, is very remote, and

[1] *Statesman Earthquake Record*, p. 7.

THE DEVASTATED AREA

a thick jungle, which covers a mountain ascent, has to be passed through before the State of Nepal can finally be reached.

When I made full inquiries some years ago about this journey into Nepal, I was told that it would necessitate travelling by means of elephants at least over one part of the journey. Whatever reconstruction, therefore, is needed will have to depend mainly on what can be obtained within the State itself. At present, singularly little news has been made public concerning what has happened in the interior of this large and fertile valley.

CHAPTER IV

WHAT SCIENCE TELLS US

i

It may be well to leave on one side for a moment the narrative of events concerning the Indian earthquake in order to find out what modern Science has to say about its causes and effects. Why did the earthquake happen in that particular spot? What was the exciting cause that made it suddenly occur at that exact moment?

The sciences of geology and meteorology are yet young, but they have made remarkable strides forward in the last few years. They may even now, therefore, be able to help us in answering these practical questions. The time may come in the not distant future when a warning may be given us that a severe earthquake is likely to happen, just as predictions are made with some exactness concerning cyclonic disturbances to-day.

As an instance which shows how sensitive the atmosphere is to earth vibration, Dr. S. N. Sen of Calcutta tells us that he was able to predict on November 5, 1930, a severe storm in the South Andamans Sea, near to Sumatra, by observing from day to day a series of microscisms (small earth shocks) on a scientific instrument in Calcutta.[1]

[1] *Statesman Earthquake Record*, p. 32.

WHAT SCIENCE TELLS US

ii

Countries like Mexico, or Italy, or Java, or Japan, are subject to earthquake shocks in certain zones because the earth-crust at those points has volcanic fires beneath it, which burst through the surface, or overflow from the craters of active volcanoes in devastating streams of lava. These eruptions are frequently accompanied by immense cracks in the earth's surface. The recent Indian earthquake was not of this character.

It was due rather to the sudden side-movement, or jerk, or dislocation, of huge rock formations far below the earth's surface. It was what geologists call "tectonic" rather than "volcanic"; that is to say, it was caused by some rock displacement, not by any great explosion below the surface.

The Himalayas, we are told, are part of a long mountain chain, whose rocks have been folded and piled up, one upon another, by a pressure brought to bear upon them from the north.

Sir Edward Pascoe explains, in what reads like a fairy story, how at one time the great Gondwana continent —as scientists call it—stretched right across to South Africa, including Madagascar and the small intervening islands as an integral part of its formation. After a colossal outpouring of molten lava through fissures in the earth's surface the continent broke up, and masses of it sank beneath the ocean, as it poured in where the earth collapsed. Relics of this sunken portion have recently been mapped out, beneath the Arabian Sea, by the "John Murray" expedition.

THE INDIAN EARTHQUAKE

"The compressional movement," Sir Edward Pascoe writes, "which initiated the Himalaya in these troublous times, persisted through the subsequent Tertiary Period, and there is good reason to believe is still in operation to-day. The rocks of the Himalaya range have been folded and contorted in the most complicated way, and have become hard and rigid with age and pressure."[1]

Those who have wandered into the recesses of the Himalayas can easily corroborate this scientific description of "folding" and contortion. We can also understand Sir Edward Pascoe's illustration of the "lateral compressional" force which brought it about.

He takes the analogy of a table napkin, which is laid out flat upon the table and then pressed inwards from two different sides at the same time. It will produce folds reaching the highest point somewhere near the centre. Where the analogy breaks down, he says, is in the fact that the piling up of rock-masses causes breaks, or "faults," while the napkin folds are continuous.

Sir Edward pictures two huge obstructive points—one at the western end of the great curve and one at the eastern corner. The lateral compressional force from the north could not bend or break these two hard points, or nodules, in the mass of molten and semi-molten rock which was being pushed up from the south. But in between them the lateral pressure from the north won in this titanic struggle. The convex or arc-like shape of the intervening Himalaya Mountains denotes this victory.

[1] "Lecture on the Indian Earthquake," Royal Society of Arts, April 13, 1934.

WHAT SCIENCE TELLS US

Along this southern foot of the Himalaya runs what is called the "Great Boundary Fault." It is here that the pressure from the north may produce at uncertain intervals, not a smooth movement which imperceptibly changes the earth formation, but a series of "jerks." It seems to be proved—at least as a good working hypothesis—that new "jerks" of this kind, at some vulnerable point in the "Great Boundary Fault," create these terribly destructive earthquake shocks in the Indo-Gangetic plain.

iii

Thus far the geologist leads us forward, and he points out from his side that the weather may have a great deal to do with the exact time at which the destructive shock occurs by changing suddenly the balance of the pressure, and thus disturbing what had always been an unsafe equilibrium.

Sir Edward takes us into the interior of the Himalayas and shows us what immense damage can be done by an excessive rain or snowfall on those tremendous slopes; how whole mountainsides in Nature's laboratories come toppling down, as they are split by frost or forced asunder by melting shows; how erosion, no less destructive, goes on all the while at lower ranges. These continuous processes may shift, by millions of tons, the mass weight of Mount Everest, or Kinchinjunga, or Nanga Parbat, in a single heavy monsoon, and thus alter the balance.

Here again amateurs, who are not scientists, can

THE INDIAN EARTHQUAKE

corroborate, from what they have seen in the interior, the terrific force of these giant weapons of Nature's armoury when they are actively at work.

Theories such as these explain the very intimate connection between the research worker in meteorology and the geological specialist. Therefore we go with some confidence to find out what Dr. S. N. Sen can tell us concerning the effect of atmospheric changes on a large scale upon the Himalayan border where the earthquake on January 15th occurred. For—to use an apt metaphor—any one of these major atmospheric effects may have "pulled the trigger" and thus brought the earthquake shock about.

He mentions three phenomena, happening near to the time of the earthquake, which may have accelerated the movement of the earth and caused the "jerk" in North Bihar.

(1) During the preceding monsoon of 1933 the rainfall was much in excess on the Kumaun Hills, which lie to the west of Bihar in the United Provinces, while the rainfall was markedly defective on the Khasi-Jaintia Hills, which lie to the east in Assam.

(2) At the end of November 1933 there was a huge earthquake below the shallow sea in Baffin Bay, North America, which was so severe that it threw completely out of gear instruments as distant as those in the British Isles. This convulsion was followed by many different minor shocks, and is supposed to have brought with it atmospheric changes of an abnormal character.

(3) Possibly, in part due to these disturbances in the

extreme North, within the Arctic Circle there was a marked wave of intense cold which passed over the whole of Northern India, starting from the West, during the week before the earthquake. This travelled along the foot-hills from the Punjab to Bengal, and produced here and there unseasonable rain.

iv

Whether all these unusual conditions accelerated the earthquake shock and brought it to a head in North Bihar cannot be scientifically proved; but as the data are collected and compared there may be in the future far greater certainty in the calculation of antecedent causes, and this may lead on even to partial prediction.

In this connection between atmosphere and earth I would call attention to that ineffaceable impression which I received at the time of the Kangra Valley Earthquake. For I can never forget, as long as I live, that cry of hundreds of birds in the early morning outside my room in Delhi when the earthquake shock occurred. It was this screaming of the birds which made me realize more than anything else what was really happening. It seemed as if they were more susceptible, even from their comparative safety, to the earthquake "atmosphere," just as one often sees them strangely disturbed before the coming of a violent thunderstorm. Their senses, which can feel the call of springtime in the North, when they are thousands of miles away in the South, may be more "tuned in" than ours.

THE INDIAN EARTHQUAKE

V

With regard to India itself, Dr. S. N. Sen gives us some general considerations which may prove of practical importance.

(1) The foot of the Himalayas is the main area of earthquake activity in India.

(2) The cold weather is more likely to give rise to earthquake conditions than the hot season.

(3) Disturbances, causing fluctuations of temperature, sometimes pass from the North-West along the foot of the Himalayas eastward, bringing with them great changes in atmospheric pressure.

If it be asked, in conclusion, whether all this laborious spade work in science carries with it any practical result, it is difficult to point immediately to a final answer. Yet even to-day, whenever great hydro-electric schemes are being planned, involving millions of pounds sterling, it becomes a serious consideration whether the locality chosen for the new power station is "earthquake proof" or not.

It may also help accurate weather-forecasting, on which agriculture more and more depends, if we are able to weigh in the balance the hitherto imponderable factor of earth disturbance and its vibration in the upper air.

We are at the beginning of a new era of scientific discovery rather than at the end. With far more sensitive instruments in our hands than our forefathers had, and new weapons, such as wireless and television, we may be able to achieve greater triumphs of accurate forecasting than have ever been dreamt of before; and in this important work the leading men of science in India, with their delicacy of touch and perception, will play an increasingly prominent part.

CHAPTER V

THE FLOODS IN ORISSA

i

IN order to understand fully the extreme plight in which the Province of Bihar and Orissa has been left by the sudden calamity on January 15, 1934, it is necessary to take into account a previous tragedy which happened in the south of the province, called Orissa, only a short time before. For the worst flood that had ever occurred during the past fifty years swept away the entire rice crop, in the Mahanadi Delta, for hundreds of square miles.

During one of the worst nights, at the height of the monsoon, while a hurricane was blowing in the Bay of Bengal, the terrible tragedy took place. Day after day, before this, the tropical rains had descended till the great river, Mahanadi, was full to overflowing. Still the deluge continued. The town of Cuttack, which lies at the head of the delta, was in danger. The townspeople anxiously watched the flood-mark on the embankment as the whirling current rushed by. The highest mark had already been over-passed, and the water had begun to pour in on the lower levels of the town where the poorest people had their huts. Then came this awful night of hurricane sweeping up from the Bay of Bengal. It seemed as if nothing could save the town.

The high tide at sea and the driving storm were

THE FLOODS IN ORISSA

forcing the huge sea waves right up the river mouth. The flood-water came pouring down from the interior. It was a battle of giants.

At last a breach was made by the raging flood in the right-hand embankment about ten miles below the town. The waters poured through. The breach became wider and wider. The pressure on the town of Cuttack was relieved, so that it soon became out of danger. But in that one night the main current of the Mahanadi, rushing through the breach, had formed a new river in its own delta, sixty miles long. This torrent of water forced its way across the standing crops, until it found an outlet into the Bay of Bengal.

ii

I shall not soon forget the experience when we went in a country boat to bring relief to some marooned people, who were on the embankment just below the breach. The Mahanadi had risen again, owing to further rains, and had almost reached its former level. Our boat was taken down the current at terrific speed, and the boatmen had difficulty in guiding it on its course. When we came to the gap, through which the Mahanadi was still pouring its flood-waters, we were first of all drawn towards the new current. Then, as we passed it in our boat, we had an equally difficult task to cross the river below the breach without being carried much farther downstream.

That very morning thirty people had been rescued by the relief workers and brought safe to the embankment. Cattle had been lost, and all the harvest had been washed

THE INDIAN EARTHQUAKE

away. The seed which had been newly sown on the chance of a "catch-crop," after the first flood had subsided, had also been destroyed.

Destitution could not go further, and the misery of the marooned villagers was heartbreaking to witness. Malaria of a malignant type and cholera soon followed in the wake of enfeebled health, due to exposure and lack of nourishing food.

iii

In all this Flood Relief work in Orissa in 1933 the Government officials and the people's representatives worked side by side in harmony together. There was no clash or over-lapping. It was proved by this practical experiment on a large scale that such close co-operation is fully possible where human lives are at stake. The sense of the urgency of the human need made difficulties vanish.

iv

It will easily be understood that a previous calamity such as this in Orissa, in the south of the same province of Bihar, has very seriously added to the difficulty of making the earthquake appeal effective.

A large number of the best volunteer workers had already offered their services for flood-relief in Orissa, and public appeals for help had been made on an extensive scale, though the response had not come up to expectation on account of the economic distress. Remissions had been granted in land revenue, and loans for rebuilding houses and sowing of seed for future crops had been offered. The Central Government of India had provided an allowance from the People's Famine Fund.

Though this relief from different quarters was far from adequate, it had already tapped the main sources of supply which are first drawn upon in any national calamity.

Then suddenly came the earthquake in the North of the same province.

The result has been twofold:

(1) It has tended to draw away from Orissa both personal and monetary help just at the time when these were most urgently needed.

(2) It has made it difficult to deal quickly with the earthquake in North Bihar on a scale commensurate with the ruin which Nature has wrought.

v

What, then, is the remedy in such a double disaster in a single province?

First of all, it is necessary to call upon the whole of India to respond with an even greater effort than any witnessed before. Without an adequate response, both in personal service and also in material things, it will not be possible to send out an effective appeal to the rest of the world.

But granted that the response has been generous beyond all that could be expected—and there is every

THE INDIAN EARTHQUAKE

sign that this has been the case—then, in the second place, India has the right, in the name of humanity, to make a further appeal to the rest of the world, as Japan did in 1923.

However hard the times may be, and however difficult it may appear to make India's voice heard amid universal disorder, this world-appeal is needed.

The "cry of the poor and destitute," about which the Psalmist writes, "must not be forgotten."

vi

One word more may be added which will echo through this book. May it not come to pass that by this constructive work of international goodwill, entirely transcending the bounds of race, religion, creed, or caste, the longing desire for world peace, which is in the heart of the mute multitudes, may be brought nearer? May not the work itself call truce to our divisions and make us all one?

By all means let us go on with every conference which may lead forward to military disarmament; but let us at the same time "disarm" fear and suspicion among the nations, overcoming these evils by loving service. And surely one of the best ways to do this, which brings with it no reaction and no regret, is the union in common work to serve suffering humanity.

CHAPTER VI

THE ALL-INDIA RESPONSE

i

As soon as ever the facts about the disaster were made known throughout the whole of India, each province sent its own volunteers and also its contribution in money and goods. Men and women were startled into action.

One noticeable feature was the way in which the women of India took up the work of relief. The Women's Movement has done much in recent years, and at this critical time its help was invaluable. Men and women worked side by side together in organizing relief, and thus an added strength was given to the cause.

India is a vast country, which is almost like a continent. Its population numbers one-fifth of the human race. On this account, when former appeals for public support have been made it has always taken a long time for the news to travel from one end of India to the other, and for the relief itself to get started. Only last year, for instance, the floods in Orissa, in spite of their phenomenal character, did not succeed in calling forth in the end an All-India response. Even the financial help was on a much lower scale than before, because of the world depression.

But the response to the earthquake appeal was quite different. No doubt it touched the imagination. There were other reasons besides, of which one was the women's

THE INDIAN EARTHQUAKE

practical concern that I have mentioned. The direct appeal of human suffering on a vast scale was brought home to the hearts of men and women in a dramatic manner, and in its most universal form. It stood entirely apart from all differences of class and creed, and made everyone conscious of an inner unity, as a people suddenly called upon to face suffering and to overcome it.

The newspaper Press of India, realizing the strength of this wave of popular feeling and sensitive to its demands, gave full space to the earthquake news, and opened at once its columns for subscriptions. To the great surprise of those who knew well the distress of the times, the response was everywhere quite unprecedented. The reply from a distant city such as Madras was in no way behind that of Calcutta and Allahabad, which had actually felt the earthquake shock.

By the end of a month nearly a hundred organizations from every part of India had either sent their representatives to work in the field or else were collecting subscriptions for the Central Fund.

ii

There is one Indian leader, Rajendra Prasad, whose name has always been associated with Bihar as its most devoted public servant. He had suffered political imprisonment as a Congress leader, and had become seriously ill in jail. At the time of the earthquake he was in hospital; but his release on the ground of ill-health had already been decided on by the Bihar Government.

On the day after the disaster he was unconditionally

THE ALL-INDIA RESPONSE

released. In spite of his ill-health, he immediately took up the relief work with a vigour which surprised his doctors most of all. He took complete charge of the local situation, and offered whole-hearted co-operation with the Bihar Government for the relief of the distressed.

"I am writing," he wrote to the Chief Secretary, "to assure you that in this humanitarian work there can be but one consideration, and that is to render such service as may be possible. It will be our privilege to assist and co-operate with other organizations, official and non-official, working for relief."

The Government replied at once, warmly accepting this generous offer of co-operation, leading on to united action.

iii

Rajendra Prasad's immediate co-operation with the Bihar Government was fully supported by Mahatma Gandhi, who placed himself at the disposal of the Bihar leader. He only asked that if possible he might be allowed to complete his tour in South India before coming north.

For a month Rajendra Prasad carried on the organizing work without summoning Mahatma Gandhi. But at last he determined to call an All-India Committee at Patna. Reference will be made to this and to Gandhi's own visit to Bihar in a later chapter.[1]

iv

From the day when Rajenda Prasad took up the public duty of Chairman of the Central Relief Committee he

[1] See Chapter VIII.

has never spared himself, but worked literally night and day with scarcely time even to eat.

If to lose the thought of self in the service of others is to find the highest life of all, then he has found it. He has also brought his whole mind to bear, as one who knows his own countrymen, on the practical problems of the future. Among the different statements regarding the building up of a New Bihar I have found his writings to stand out in a class by themselves. For he has proved himself to be an original thinker, not merely dealing with the immediate problem of human suffering, but also planning a forward-looking programme of reconstruction.

He has been careful, from the very first, to set his face like a flint against any doles of money, which pauperize those who receive them and weaken their inner character. In every way he has been specially on his guard to maintain the self-respect and initiative of those who have to face a hard, uphill battle with harsh outward circumstances, if they are to come through this terrible ordeal unscathed.

V

One frail and infirm All-India leader, much older than Rajendra Prasad, but sharing to the full his invincible courage, is the Vice-Chancellor of the Hindu University, Pundit Madan Mohan Malaviya. He has sent from Benares, which is near at hand, those young men among his students who were available for immediate relief work. While he himself is past the age of active social service, his inspiration has been felt by all.

THE ALL-INDIA RESPONSE

The Musalmans have united with the Hindus in this work of public duty. One who is growing old in years, Maulana Abul Kalam Azad, has constantly rendered personal service when any occasion arose and has never spared himself in action. Other Muslim leaders have done the same.

vi

The inclusive and representative character of the Committee has been shown by appointing as one of its Vice-Presidents the Hon. Husain Imam, a non-official member of the Council of State. Mr. C. H. Holmes, representing the mercantile community of Calcutta, has also taken active part both in visiting the devastated area and as a member of the Central Relief Committee. The two secretaries, S. M. Hafeez and Baldeo Sahai, have been chosen from the two major religious communities of the province.

Among the societies which have been most active in Relief work, mention may be made of the Marwari Relief Society, the Ramkrishna Mission, the Servants of India Society, and the Memon Relief Society. Sabarmati Asram has sent a valuable contingent of workers. Other societies also have done excellent work, but the list is too long for special mention in a book of this kind.

vii

Among the All-India leaders the very first to go forward into the devastated area, in order to render personal

THE INDIAN EARTHQUAKE

service, was Jawaharlal Nehru. He led a party of workers, and helped to clear away the *débris*, and also to organize relief parties at a most critical time when immediate action was needed.

Just as general satisfaction was expressed when Rajendra Prasad was released, so there was great disappointment everywhere expressed when Jawaharlal Nehru was prosecuted and imprisoned.[1] For this happened just when the Government and people appeared to be drawing nearer together in a common humanitarian work. It was generally felt that a great opportunity of showing goodwill had been lost.

viii

The first three cables to reach me in England concerning the extent of the disaster were from Rabindranath Tagore, Mahatma Gandhi, and Rajendra Prasad.

The cable from the Poet brought home to me what he rightly called the "staggering news" concerning the vastness of what had happened. In all three messages I was asked to make the appeal as wide as possible for sympathy and help.

At first it was necessary to remain in England in order to make the facts adequately known. After that a tour was arranged for me covering the chief cities in Northern and Western Europe. After this I was obliged to fulfil

[1] Jawaharlal Nehru was convicted, on February 16, 1933, of "sedition" under S. 124a of the Indian Penal Code, in respect of certain public speeches delivered in Bengal on January 17th and 18th, and he was sentenced to two years' simple imprisonment.

THE ALL-INDIA RESPONSE

a previous engagement to go to South Africa. Wherever I went, it saddened me to find that the news about the extent of the Indian earthquake had almost passed unnoticed.

During all those months of varied experience the need of a short book, making known the facts, had been constantly pressed upon me, and I had prepared a manuscript for the press. But before it could be published the further news of the floods in the devastated area had been cabled out from India. Therefore it seemed best to wait, until I had personally visited North Bihar and considered the whole question of the future on the spot after consultation with Rajendra Prasad and others.

On account of ill-health in India I was not able to fulfil the whole of this programme, or to stay in the flood-stricken area, but I was able to spend some time at the headquarters of the Central Relief Committee at Patna, going into the details of what was happening, and carrying away for further study different reports. Furthermore, I was able to stay with Rajendra Prasad not only at Patna but also at Wardha, and to meet other Indian leaders who had taken active part in Earthquake Relief.

CHAPTER VII

HOW GOVERNMENT ACTED

i

IT is not easy in the West to realize what an all-important part the official Government of India plays, not only in great public matters but also in local affairs. The constant use of the word "Government" (Sarkar), without the definite article, is a small but significant indication of this very thing.

By a long series of changes, during last century, the details of administration became more and more concentrated in official hands. The average villager was content to pay his dues and allow this process to go on. Thus the tendency grew apace.

Far-sighted administrators, however, like Lord Ripon, along with the wisest Indian statesmen, perceived the inherent weakness of such a process. Therefore the attempt was made to introduce local self-government in various ways. During recent years this policy has been much more seriously pressed forward, and the active principle contained in it lies at the back of all the new constitutional proposals. It also accounts for the intense earnestness and determination behind the great National Movement while it seeks to realize self-rule.

These factors have a direct bearing on the problem of earthquake relief, though the political aspect will

HOW GOVERNMENT ACTED

naturally be kept in the background in a book of this character.

Looking at what is immediately feasible, from a purely humanitarian standpoint, it is clear to everyone on the spot, official and non-official alike, that not only is it not practical at this crisis, caused by the earthquake, for the local government to withdraw its powers, but on the contrary those powers must be increased in certain important directions.

For instance, Government must stop all profiteering by drastic action. It must issue new loans at the lowest rate of interest; it must also remit taxation. It may have to undertake new town and village planning on a large scale. It may also have to exercise strict medical control over large areas in order to prevent epidemics, which spread like wildfire in India if once they get started. All these things will be expected of Government by the people, and it will be judged according to its ability to carry through such measures.

Yet if Government is wise and considerate it will welcome at the same time, with open arms, all voluntary effort, and will make its appeal to every movement among the people towards self-help and self-recovery.

For the area of suffering is so vast that the greatest danger ahead will be that of apathy leading to despair. To be merely passive recipients of Government bounty; to sit back and let Government do everything—this would lead to a disaster greater than the earthquake itself, for it would sap all moral courage.

Therefore the voluntary organization can render

THE INDIAN EARTHQUAKE

invaluable assistance, for its enthusiasm and energy create a new hope among the sufferers, as I have personally witnessed among the flood-stricken people in Orissa.

What I have written is based on a long experience of the difficulties that arise when Government officials and voluntary workers carry on their public service side by side. Conflicts have arisen in quite recent years which have injured the common cause and added to the sufferings of the poor.

ii

The Report presented by the Bihar Government to the Legislative Council relates in detail how the vastness of the sudden calamity took everyone by surprise. All communication (as we have seen) with the northern side of the Ganges was cut off. Out of nine hundred miles of rail, hardly a mile of track remained undamaged. Rails remained suspended in mid air; bridges were twisted out of shape and broken down. The city of Patna itself, the centre of the province, from which all orders had to be sent to the districts, suffered severely. At first, confusion could hardly be avoided. Many were killed and injured, and most of the Government buildings were badly shaken. It was itself an earthquake-stricken city.

Shocks of a minor character were still going on during the night of January 15th and early on the next morning. Much had to be done in the city to prevent panic, but by the morning of January 16th order reigned.

News from Muzaffarpur, across the Ganges, had to

HOW GOVERNMENT ACTED

be brought in by hand by a messenger who travelled on foot through the night and reached Patna on the morning of January 16th. The first news of all came from Monghyr. A telegram was despatched on the night of January 15th from the Commissioner at Bhagalpur concerning Monghyr, which reached Government at Patna the next morning. A party of four doctors and five senior medical students was despatched on the morning of January 16th to Monghyr, and seven Public Health doctors started for Muzaffarpur on the morning of January 17th.

At midday on January 16th the Government telegraphed to Calcutta for two aeroplanes. At 5 p.m. on the 16th an aeroplane belonging to "Captain Barnard's Circus" unexpectedly reached Patna. It had flown earlier in the day over Muzaffarpur, where Mr. Fairweather, an experienced pilot and engineer, had managed to mark out a strip of ground for its landing. He had chalked out also an S O S, and had signalled to the pilot as he flew quite low. The aeroplane landed with some difficulty and took Mr. Fairweather on board. They made that day an air reconnaissance over a large part of the stricken area, as far as Motihari, and afterwards reached Patna the same evening, January 16th.

This aeroplane was kept over January 17th, and a second aeroplane, belonging to the Indian Air Survey, arrived from Calcutta on that date. This was used on January 18th to take the Governor over the whole stricken area. Other aeroplanes came, including a private plane belonging to Mr. Matthews. Thus a work of reconnaissance, which would have taken many days to accomplish by road—with bridges destroyed and open fissures in all directions—was accomplished in a few hours from the air.

iii

Instead of following out the different items, which are given in the Government reports, it may be best to give in detail the immediate measures taken at one or two centres, which are typical.

The District Officer at Monghyr escaped with his life, and saw at once that the Civil Surgeon's house and the jail wall had collapsed. He found, however, to his great relief, that the Civil Surgeon, with his wife and children, had all escaped. But the Superintendent of the Police had been badly injured, and was being taken to the hospital. The jailer, with great presence of mind, had secured 280 prisoners in a shed, and none had escaped. An armed guard was put over them, and all available police, with their officers, were sent at once to the bazaar for rescue work.

Roads and lanes were completely indistinguishable owing to the heap of ruins, and it was difficult to know where to go first to rescue those who might still be alive. From a portion of the main road, within twelve yards, as many as forty dead bodies were recovered.

Monghyr is on the south side of the River Ganges, and railway communication had been rapidly restored. On January 20th a magnificent act of private charity was performed by Messrs. Tata Iron & Steel Co., Ltd., which worthily upheld the record for munificence which the Parsee

HOW GOVERNMENT ACTED

community has always maintained. They sent a special train, with workmen, which carried 120 tons of iron sheets, five trucks of rice, together with mechanics and tools to Monghyr. These at once began putting up hospital sheds and other buildings.

Four relief centres were organized in the town for distribution of food, blankets, etc., with medical aid attached to each. Dr. Mukharji and Mr. Bhide started a sanitation centre, and by January 24th the Red Cross Hospital unit had arrived from Calcutta.

One of the serious dangers, in a disaster of such magnitude as this, was lest pilfering and looting might begin on a large scale. Things that would disgrace the district might be easily done, if once law and order broke down and men of evil character were abroad.

"Actually," the report runs, "the menace of looting came to nothing. . . . There was almost a total absence of crime of this character. The extra police, therefore, which had been called in, were able to render whatever immediate assistance might be required. They were in the forefront of rescue work. The only Government servants who lost their lives through the earthquake belonged to the police."

iv

The town of Motihari, which lies far to the north, may be taken as an example of a distant place where conditions of providing relief were far more difficult. It was entirely cut off by road, rail, and telegraph. "Motihari," says the

THE INDIAN EARTHQUAKE

Finance Member, "has suffered more than almost any other place. It is only because of its wide streets that the death-roll was not a much heavier one. The people were able to escape into the open. Sober men, with all their wits about them, who were engaged half an hour later in rescue work, almost believed that the end of the world had come, and that the whole solid earth was breaking up beneath their feet. I cannot attempt to describe it. The whole town was shattered, and we believe now that it will be impossible to build it again on the same site."

The Collector acted with promptness. He sent out a gang at once to try to repair the telegraph line, and called a public meeting in order to map out the immediate work to be done.

At two o'clock on the next afternoon the aeroplane from "Captain Barnard's Circus" flew overhead. This was the first communication from the outer world. On the 17th another aeroplane dropped a message that further police help was on the way. Food prices were fixed and published, and all arrangements were made to hold out for a few days with their own resources until road transport should be restored.

On January 18th the Collector reported that the state of the town had improved. The open gaps in the main road had been filled up, and dangerous houses had been demolished. By the energy of Mr. Vakil, the District Engineer, all the important roads had been made passable by January 21st.

HOW GOVERNMENT ACTED

v

More than two months later Mr. G. K. Devadhar, President of the Servants of India Society, visited the same area. He had himself, in earlier years, organized relief work on a large scale in Malabar, after the Moplah Rebellion, and therefore could give a good estimate of what had been accomplished. He found all the voluntary agencies, which were grouped under the Central Relief Committee, working in admirable accord with the Government officials.

"It is remarkable to observe," he reports, "from talks with the officers of Government, non-official agencies, and people personally affected, how valiantly they are struggling with the situation and trying their utmost to meet the demands of the various problems created by it with the resources at their command. We had talks with groups of people in towns and villages, and it was encouraging to find that they were bearing the calamity with great fortitude.

"The people are full of hope that both the Government and the rest of the country will come to their rescue, and will give help that will go a long way to restore the normal life of the province."

vi

In India itself the Viceroy's Earthquake Relief Fund was immediately started, and a Government appeal was made to the whole of India which brought in over £444,000, bringing the total voluntary subscriptions collected from all sources to about £750,000.

CHAPTER VIII

THE MORAL PROBLEM

i

IT happened that, in the first days which followed the earthquake, when minds were stunned by the awfulness of the calamity, the whole problem of human suffering and divine chastisement was raised in the public Press by Mahatma Gandhi himself. India would hardly be true to her past tradition, as the country where religion counts most of all, if this issue had not been faced in a public manner.

It was brought forward in a great argument; and two national representatives—Gandhi and Tagore—entered the lists for the debate.

"I am being crushed to pieces," Mahatma Gandhi had written, "by the thought of this disaster. Yet I talk, laugh, seem to enjoy—for I have to do that. But in reality I am thinking of this appalling calamity all the twenty-four hours."

He had already encountered, as he went further South, the unspeakably cruel selfishness of man which could go on perpetrating the sin of "untouchability." His mind was steeped in that problem. Now suddenly he was confronted with the calamity of North Bihar.

"These two things," he wrote to a friend, "more than fill my thoughts, and I am constantly seeking God's guidance."

THE MORAL PROBLEM

He immediately called a solemn truce and a cessation of controversy both within the ranks of Indians themselves and also with Government.

"This divine calamity," he declared at Tuticorin, "has suddenly reminded us that all humanity is one; and, as is but right and proper in the face of this calamity, the Government and the people have become one. For the time being, distinctions between Congress and non-Congress, between Congress and Government, have been abolished."

On every possible occasion he repeated this central message and acted upon it.

ii

Then he went much further and began to probe into the mystery of the dreadful calamity, which he himself had called "divine." He attempted

> To justify the ways of God to man,

and it is a matter of profound interest to follow the workings of his mind thus abnormally excited and active.

He takes a strange course in doing so, which most of us in the West find hard to pursue with him, though we can feel in his utterance the voice of a prophet in the wilderness speaking out of the storm and tempest of his own troubled spirit, and seeking with tragic earnestness to hear the "still, small voice" within.

"I want you everyone," he cries aloud, "to be superstitious enough with me to believe that this disaster is

THE INDIAN EARTHQUAKE

a divine chastisement for the great sin we have committed, and are still committing, against those whom *we* call 'untouchables,' but *I* have called 'God's children'! ... Our earthly existence is so fickle that, as this disaster shows, we may be wiped out in the twinkling of an eye. Therefore, while we have time, let us repent! Let us get rid of all distinctions of high and low in the sight of God! Let us purify our hearts and be ready to face our Maker."

"I know," he cried again, "you are all believers in God! Our forefathers have taught us to think that when a great calamity comes it is because of our personal sin.

"You know that when rain does not come we perform sacrifices and ask God to forgive us our sins. It is not only here, but in England and in South Africa also I have seen it, that when, for instance, locusts descend upon the fields, or any such thing happens, they appoint days of humiliation, prayer, and fasting. So I want you to believe with me that for this absolutely unthinkable affliction in Bihar your sins and my sins are responsible!

"I ask myself," he went on, "what that sin can be to warrant such a calamity. The conviction is growing upon me that this calamity has come upon us on account of the atrocious sin of untouchability.... I am not given to appealing to the superstitious fears of men, but I cannot help telling you what is going on deep down in my heart to-day."

In his written article he goes still further. "I share the belief," he writes, "with the whole world—civilized and

THE MORAL PROBLEM

uncivilized—that calamities, such as the Bihar one, come to mankind as chastisement for their sins. When that conviction comes from the heart, people pray, repent, and purify themselves. I regard untouchability as such a grave sin as to warrant divine chastisement. I am not affected by posers such as 'Why punishment to Bihar and not to the South?' (where untouchability is worst) or "Why an earthquake, and not some other form of punishment?' I am not God. Therefore I have but a limited knowledge of His purpose.

"Such calamities are not a mere caprice of the Deity, or Nature. They obey fixed laws as surely as the planets do. Only we do not know the laws governing them. Whatever, therefore, may be said about them must be regarded as guesswork. But guessing has a definite place in a man's life. It is an ennobling thing to me to think that the Bihar disturbance is due to the sin of untouchability. It makes me humble. It spurs me on to greater effort towards its removal. It encourages me to purify myself. It brings me nearer to my Maker.

"That my guess may be wrong does not affect the results named by me. For what is a guess to the sceptic or critic is a living belief with me, and I base my future actions on that belief. Such guesses become superstitious only when they lead to no purification.

"But such misuse of divine events cannot deter men of faith from interpreting them as a call to them for repentance of their sins. I do not interpret this chastisement as an exclusive punishment for the sin of untouchability. It is open to others to read in it divine wrath against many other sins. But let reformers regard the earthquake as a nemesis for the sin of untouchability. They cannot go wrong if they have the faith that I have. They will help Bihar more and not less for that faith. And they will try to produce an atmosphere against the reproduction of untouchability in any scheme of reconstruction."

iii

This declaration, uttered day after day, and repeated in all the newspapers, drew an indignant moral protest from the poet, Rabindranath Tagore, who wrote as follows:

"It has caused me painful surprise to find Mahatma Gandhi accusing those who blindly follow their own social custom of untouchability for having brought down God's vengeance upon certain parts of Bihar, evidently specially selected for His desolating displeasure! It is all the more unfortunate, because this unscientific and materialistic view of things is too readily accepted by large sections of our countrymen.

"I keenly feel the indignity of it when I am compelled to utter the truism that physical catastrophies have their inevitable and exclusive origin in a certain combination of physical facts. Unless we believe in the inexorableness of universal laws, in the working of which God Himself never interferes, imperilling thereby the integrity of His own creation, we find it impossible to justify His ways on occasions like the one which has so sorely stricken us in an overwhelming manner and scale.

THE MORAL PROBLEM

"If we associate the ethical principles with cosmic phenomena we shall have to admit that human nature is morally superior to a Providence that preaches lessons on good behaviour in orgies of the worst behaviour possible. For we can never imagine any civilized ruler of man making indiscriminate examples of casual victims, including children and members of the untouchable community themselves, in order to impress others dwelling at a safe distance who possibly deserve severer condemnation.

"Though we cannot point to any period of human history that is free from iniquities of the darkest kind, we still find citadels of malevolence that remain unshaken; factories that cruelly thrive upon the poverty and ignorance of famished cultivators. It only shows that the law of gravitation does not in the least respond to the stupendous load of callousness that accumulates till the moral foundations of our society begin to show dangerous cracks and civilizations are undermined.

"What is truly tragic is the fact that the argument Mahatma Gandhi used, by exploiting an event of cosmic disturbance, far better suits the psychology of his opponents than his own; and it would not have surprised me if they had taken the opportunity of holding him and his followers responsible for the visitation of divine anger. As for us, we feel perfectly secure in the faith that our own sins and errors, however enormous, have not got enough force to drag down the structure of Creation to ruin.

"We, who are immensely grateful to Mahatma Gandhi

for inducing by his wonderful inspiration freedom from fear and feebleness in the minds of our countrymen, feel profoundly hurt when any words from his mouth may emphasize elements of unreason in those very minds—that unreason which is the fundamental source of all blind powers that drive us against freedom and self-respect."

iv

Probably in rural India, with its whole heart and mind continually set upon these ultimate problems of the Divine in Nature and Man, this moral issue raised by Mahatma Gandhi and rebutted by Rabindranath Tagore will go on reverberating long after the shocks of the Bihar Earthquake have ceased to rumble below the ground. For there is always in the Indian village mind an irresistible urge to go on seeking to penetrate further into the mysteries of that Divine Nature in which we live and move and have our being. The profoundest of all religious conceptions have come in India from villagers like Kabir and Dadu, and countless unknown village minds which have expressed themselves in song. Tagore himself had written about the Bauls of his own Bengal, and translated into English some of their immortal verse.

In other lands the long line of seers and prophets goes back as far as the Book of Job, and much further still. The modern questioning of Thomas Hardy's *Dynasts*, and the startling Romanes Lecture of Huxley, with his terrible simile of the Chess Player with whom

THE MORAL PROBLEM

we are to play the Game of Life, show us that the problem is by no means solved.

But here I would leave the words of the two great Indian prophets, so strangely differing in their outlook, and yet each representing one aspect of the Indian background. It appears to me, as I look on, that there was a vital issue which forced each of them to speak in turn. For Tagore was surely right in confronting Gandhi with the baneful effect which this superstitious terror of Divine Wrath has had upon the Indian village mind. He is right in pointing out that ordinary natural phenomena, which merely obey the law of gravitation, have too often been the objects of blind fear leading on to cruelty and terror.

The propitiation of an angry God, who demands even human sacrifices and tortures in order to cause the rain to fall and the seed to ripen, has not been uncommon in pagan days in the West as well as in the East, and the superstition still lingers in crude form in every part of the world. It is an evil heritage of the race, not entirely got rid of even by civilized man himself. Horrible torments of the human body, too ghastly to describe, are still performed in order to secure such propitiation.

This "element of unreason," as Tagore rightly points out, has held sway long enough, enslaving men's minds, and it has been the great inspiration of Gandhi hitherto to break this bondage, not to bind it faster.

And yet there is a vital truth, which Tagore himself would recognize, in what Gandhi was feeling as a fire burning in his own breast. Our little minds are only stung to greatness by some great issue. Shakespeare's well-known lines—

> When beggars die there are no comets seen,
> The heavens themselves blaze forth the death of princes,

may have no scientific justification, and may be proved to be entirely irrelevant to Caesar's death, yet they go on being quoted age after age and have become proverbial, not because they embody some "element of unreason," but rather because a tragic element of majesty and awe, akin to both greatness and pity, is found in them.

The "numinous" in human life and experience may be very hard to define, but it has in it the soul of religion. It is not explicable by reason, but it is not irrational.

If, therefore, Gandhi, in his great argument with Tagore, sought to exploit a deep human sentiment and to raise it to solemn issues, such as the removal of the curse of untouchability from mankind, there may be something to be said on his side also.

A remarkable saying of Christ has been preserved in St. Luke's Gospel which appears to illustrate the argument in question. Some disaster had evidently occurred in Jerusalem, and human lives had been forfeited. Some people regarded this as a punishment for those special persons' sins. But Christ rejected that interpretation.

"Those eighteen men," He says, "on whom the tower of Siloam fell, think ye that they were sinners above all men that dwelt in Jerusalem? I tell you, Nay; but except ye repent, ye shall all likewise perish."

THE MORAL PROBLEM

Here the purely accidental in the disaster is fully recognized. It is not made an "Act of God," as old English law books might have called it. But the awe and solemnity of death in such a terrible form is not lost sight of by the young Prophet of Nazareth. "Except ye repent," says Jesus, "ye shall all likewise perish."

CHAPTER IX

MAHATMA GANDHI IN BIHAR

i

WE have already seen how, when the earthquake had suddenly brought ruin to North Bihar, Mahatma Gandhi was working in South India, where the evil of untouchability—the curse of the "pariah,"[1]—is more cruelly practised than in any other part of India. His first instinct, as he has told us, was to abandon everything else and go to the help of the distressed. But he saw at once that this was a temptation which had to be resisted.

Some who had already been to visit the earthquake zone and had been horrified by what they had seen wrote to him indignant letters, chiding him for his delay. They called the work which he was doing in the South "fiddling while Bihar was burning."

But this did not turn him from his purpose. He went on steadily forward with his effort to break down the curse of untouchability at its most vulnerable point. In the extreme South of India he was in the very citadel of the great evil, and he determined not to leave the field until he had done his work.

Yet all the while it was clear from the articles which

[1] This is undoubtedly the greatest curse in the whole of India which needs to be removed. No one has been able to make such a definite impression in the direction of its removal as Mahatma Gandhi.

MAHATMA GANDHI IN BIHAR

he wrote in his own weekly paper, called *Harijan*, that his mind was abnormally excited and disturbed. He was trying to work out, as we have seen, the age-long problem of human suffering and Divine chastisement.

Then at last, to his intense relief, he received a letter from Rajendra Prasad asking him as soon as posible to give up a whole month to a tour of the distressed area, combining it with work for the removal of untouchability in that region.

Immediately he set out on his journey northward and reached Patna, the centre of all the relief work, on the night of March 11th, nearly two months after the earthquake shock had occurred.

He had always held the affection of the Bihar and Orissa Province because of his frequent visits. On different occasions he had spent much time in Orissa, where the poverty is indescribably great. Furthermore, in the year 1917 he had gone to Champaran, in North Bihar, in order to champion the cause of the peasants. Therefore when he came back among them again his reception was almost pathetic in the depth of its enthusiastic devotion.

A remarkable sketch of what his tour meant to these earthquake-stricken people reached me in England from Miss Agatha Harrison, who knew well the condition of the masses in China and Japan as well as in India itself. She wrote to me:

"The poverty of Bihar is very well known to you. To have an earthquake on the top of this—to say nothing of the further damage that the monsoon will cause—

THE INDIAN EARTHQUAKE

baffles description. A remark made to me stays in my mind. It was said that the poverty of the men and women was at zero: the earthquake had divided this by ten.

"I am not going to describe the havoc I saw in this letter. Vivid accounts have already reached you. I would only say that I passed through Japan after the 1923 earthquake; and there is no doubt in my own mind that this is the greater disaster.

"How can I describe these days to you? With the exception of a few miles of route in the outlying districts we drove between 'walls' of people. As we neared a village or town these human walls would press in almost to the point of suffocation in an effort to see this much-loved man—Mahatma Gandhi. Sometimes through sheer fatigue he would curl up on the back seat and sleep and I would talk with Rajendra Prasad. As we neared a village, and the motor slowed down, Rajendra Prasad on one side, and the chauffeur on the other, would lean out and call out softly in Hindustani, 'He sleeps.' These words would be echoed by the people. But even this did not deter them from pressing around the car, though quite quietly, in an effort to see Mr. Gandhi. From my vantage-point I saw the expressions on their faces, and was dumb. For it was as though they had seen a god.

"Our days were punctuated by meetings at which Mr. Gandhi, and often Rajendra Prasad, would speak. I thought I knew something of crowds. But I have never seen anything like the surge of people at these meetings. Often on the edge of the crowds there would be a fringe of elephants bearing, to my mind, a far too heavy burden

MAHATMA GANDHI IN BIHAR

of people—so great was the anxiety to see this apostle of non-violence. At these gatherings either Rajendra Prasad or one of the Relief workers would give me a running interpretation of what Mr. Gandhi said. He never commiserated with them in their misery, but presented them with a challenge. 'What has this calamity taught you? This is no time for differences between Government and Congress; between Hindu and Muslim; between Touchable and Untouchable. If you take money from the Relief Funds—see that you earn it,' etc.

"And to the women, many of whom as you know are in purdah in Bihar, Mr. Gandhi would say: 'Has this calamity taught you nothing? Why this foolishness? (purdah). There is no place for purdah, except that of the heart. . . .'

"He was severely practical too. For even in this stricken area he would take a collection at every meeting, and each time we slowed down or stopped at a railway station. From the women he collected pieces of their jewellery.

"We also met with the members of the local relief committees. The burden of what Mr. Gandhi said at these times was that no agency, whether it be Government or Congress, could cope single-handed with the earthquake situation. That it needed perfectly co-ordinated effort of all. And that co-operation to be real must be tendered freely and whole-heartedly, not grudgingly or haltingly. What could be more absurd than to talk of non-co-operation to a man dying of thirst? Should he refuse water from a well sunk by the Government? Non-co-operation did not exclude humanity, common sense, or discrimination.

"Over and above all this the tour gave me the opportunity I had long wanted of meeting some of the outstanding Congress leaders, and of getting to know that loved and respected figure—Rajendra Prasad. You have often spoken to me about him, and now I can count him as a friend.

"Your cable saying that Pierre Cérésole is coming has just arrived, and has caused quite a sensation. For his coming will symbolize the 'caring' of a world outside."

What follows will be taken from the different newspaper accounts of the same tour. It will show not only the suffering of the people, but also their patient courage in face of extreme adversity.

ii

The day after Mahatma Gandhi arrived at Patna was his day of silence, which he faithfully observes every week without speaking a word to anyone for any purpose. The people flocked in thousands round the house where he was staying, and came also to the evening prayer, which is open to all.

On the next day he tried to see something of the destruction wrought in Patna city, but the crowds were so great as to make it impossible even to get down from the motor-car in which he was being taken round. On Wednesday, March 14th, Rajendra Prasad went with him to Motihari, where he had lived during the Champaran struggle, making it his headquarters. The motor road, when the Ganges was crossed, was still very rough and broken. On the way they stopped at Lalganj, with a population of nearly ten thousand. The cracked and crumbling buildings drew forth from the party exclamations of wonder, but they were told that this was only a moderately damaged town.

They started off again in order to reach Motihari, which was sixty miles away, before nightfall. On account of the cracked roads they could only go very slowly indeed. It took them over seven hours to accomplish the journey.

At one place the village people had gathered in a dense crowd, and he gave them the following message in Hindi:

"There is one thing I want to say to you. Those of you who are getting work from the Central Relief Committee are in honour bound to work well. Do good, honest work; and you who are not already working should do so. To give money for bad work, or for no work at all, is to make beggars. We do not want to turn India into a land of beggars. And you must put away untouchability from your hearts and lives."

Just as darkness was coming on they began to enter the tracts damaged by water and sand. Here the road became very bad indeed. At one place they were confronted suddenly by a mound of earth with a warning that a bridge was down. They had to make a detour across the fields and over a temporary bridge, which almost gave way under them. They had not gone far when the same thing happened again. At last they reached

THE INDIAN EARTHQUAKE

Motihari dead-tired long after nightfall, and thankful to get there in safety.

iii

The next morning they were off at six o'clock to see the countryside. They had three rivers with ferries to cross in twenty-five miles, and then came back through what had once been fields. But deserts of sand now met their eyes on every side, and even where there was a standing crop it had been blighted by the sand. The land everywhere had been perforated with craters. The water had by that time dried up, but the sand remained. It was lying everywhere like a heavy fall of snow, very fine and glistening, and almost white where the sunlight played upon it.

Nothing moved them more than the sight of this devastation. Cities, crumbled to a heap of ruins, were certainly more spectacular; yet city life can be built up again. But when the fields were destroyed, the very roots of human life were withered and dried up.

Everywhere as they passed along the road, or stayed for a few moments in order to look at some immense upheaval, the crowd collected, and the cry of "Gandhi Maharaj ki jai" rang out as the villagers tried to shout their welcome.

When he spoke at all, it was always the same message, "Work! Work! Do not beg, but work! Ask for work to do, and do it faithfully." He felt as if life itself depended on the miserable mendicant attitude being checked at the very outset.

MAHATMA GANDHI IN BIHAR

As he passed along and saw the water channels silted up with sand, it seemed to him that floods could only be avoided by a miracle happening. There was just one hope left, that the floods of rain might sweep away some of the deserts of sand which covered the soil.

iv

There were already over ten thousand people employed by the Central Relief Committee in one district alone through which he passed. The wages were incredibly low—three-halfpence a day for a man, one penny for a woman, and a halfpenny for a child. The work which was given to them was that of clearing away the sand. The fact that men, women, and children were ready to come and work at such a rate of wages revealed what a pitiable plight the villagers had reached, and how near they were to famine conditions.

On their way back to Motihari they were taken to see the worst fissures. One was deep and broad enough to contain a dozen or more elephants within its yawning chasm. Besides the fissures and the craters and the sand-blocked waterways the land had bulged up in other places, upsetting all the previous levels. In others there had been a sinking of the soil which could be equally disastrous when the rains came.

During the afternoon they went round the town of Motihari. It was broken and twisted and shapeless beyond all repair. Almost every house was damaged. Some houses were hanging together as if by a thread, and many

THE INDIAN EARTHQUAKE

were completely sunk in one large mass of rubble. The distortions of the earth under the town were something that could not even be imagined, had they not been visible before the eyes.

In one place the ground had cracked wide open, leaving the patches of soil, between the cracks, tipped this way and that like the decks of ships in a rough sea. In another place the house had cracked in two, but not fallen, as the soil on which each half stood had been moved bodily along. At another spot, a piece of wall, sticking out from the earth at an angle, was the only remains of a whole house which had vanished underground! The city of Motihari, with its beautiful site on the edge of a small lake, was ruined beyond repair.

V

On the evening of this visit all the representatives of the different Relief Committees, including the Government officials, gathered together for a conference in Motihari. Each gave in turn an account of the activities of his organization. The longest time was naturally taken up with the Government representatives, since they had the largest funds at their disposal, and the heaviest duties to fulfil.

Mahatma Gandhi expressed great pleasure at seeing the cordial co-operation, and expressed the earnest hope that this would increase and become stronger, since the magnitude of the work was such that unless there was full co-operation amongst all the workers it would be impossible to cope with the devastation.

MAHATMA GANDHI IN BIHAR

When the conference was over, a heart-to-heart talk was continued among the different non-official leaders with regard to co-operation and united action. Mahatma Gandhi pointed out that it was their bounden duty in order to help the sufferers in their uttermost needs to study the work and capacity of all other relief organizations, especially that of the Government, and to fit their own work in by taking up those cases where prompt action was required in order to save a perilous situation.

The Central Relief Committee, he pointed out, was a mobile body, with great powers of free initiative, whereas for the Government machinery it was wellnigh impossible even with the best will in the world to move with alacrity. This fact threw all the greater responsibility on the people's Committee to deal promptly with emergency cases.

vi

The party then went on to examine the different model dwellings which were being put up as an experiment with a view ultimately to house the destitute middle class which had suffered most. One model had been designed by Government officers, another had been planned by the Mayor of Calcutta's relief party. There were many suggestions to be made before any one plan was finally adopted.

One of the writers, from whom I am quoting, had lived for some time, in earlier days, in Muzaffarpur.

"I simply could not recognize the city," she relates, "though I knew it so well! Ruins all round! Soon the

THE INDIAN EARTHQUAKE

motor was unable to go further. We scrambled along the *débris* of littered roads and lanes. All the houses were laid low without exception. We came to a place where a fine old family house had once stood, in which I had stayed during my last visit to the city. I could not even tell which road I was in, nor where the front door was through which I used to pass. Nineteen persons were inside when that house collapsed. Seven of the ladies and children and three servants were killed, and six were injured. One of the children's bodies took five days to remove, and another eleven days. This is but a sample of what has happened to hundreds and hundreds of families."

When the crowd had collected, Mahatma Gandhi made the following speech:

"This is no time for talking. I have come to see and help you, and not to talk. But there are just two things I want to say to you. The first is this. The Relief Committees have the money, and either beggars or workers will take it. *I want no beggars*. It would be deplorable if this earthquake turned us into mendicants. Only those without eyes, or hands, or feet, or otherwise unfit for work may ask for alms. For the able-bodied to beg is, in the language of the Gita, for them to become thieves.

"The second thing is this, that God has Himself sent us this gift. We must accept it as a gift from Him, and then we shall understand its meaning. What is that meaning? It is this, that untouchability must go: that is to say, nobody must regard himself higher than another.

"If we can understand these two things, this earthquake will be turned into a blessing. At present we count it as a sorrow, and no wonder when we see these fair fields and lands devastated. But I pray to God that He may give us strength to make a blessing out of this destruction."

This speech Mahatma Gandhi repeated from place to place, just as he also repeated his injunction about co-operation with Government officials.

Three things stand out as obviously necessary if the critical situation is to be met:

(*a*) It is quite certain that the present resources, both of workers and also of funds, are merely touching the surface of the disaster. Where millions of pounds sterling are needed, the help so far collected has only amounted to a few hundreds of thousands. The appeal must be made in wider circles, and it must touch the heart of the world.

(*b*) No adequate relief will be possible without perfect co-operation between the Government officials and the volunteer relief associations.

(*c*) On the part of Government there needs to be full and generous treatment in the shape of loans, without interest in some cases, or with very small interest in other cases, accompanied by large remissions of taxation.

vii

We are able to trace out, as we read the different narratives of Mahatma Gandhi's visit, the main conditions which are required for successful relief work. In all the

THE INDIAN EARTHQUAKE

personal letters which have reached me from Rajendra Prasad the same two points are emphasized. They may be summarized briefly as:

(*a*) No pauperization.
(*b*) Co-operation between Government and people.

It would be very difficult to estimate the extraordinary value of a personality such as Mahatma Gandhi at such a crisis as this. It has been not unusual to report in the newspapers of Europe and America that since he has taken up the cause of the depressed classes, whom he calls "God's children,"[1] his popularity has been diminished among the illiterate villagers of India. The truth, which can easily be proved by facts and figures, is just the opposite. In a manner which was altogether unexpected, his influence instead of being diminished has increased in an amazing degree.

The very same phenomena which met him in South India have been experienced in his northern tour in Bihar. The crowds which came to hear him have been literally overwhelming.

Since he has at last determined to carry through a step he had contemplated for many years, namely, to make no use of motor-cars while he is in the country, but walk from village to village on foot, his contact with the village people, whom he understands and loves, will become closer still, and his fame is likely to increase.

One thing should surely be demanded from all sides in face of the incredible distress of these millions of poorest people. It is that there should be a truce to all

[1] Harijans.

disputes on other matters, as far as it is humanly possible, until these sufferers have been relieved.

viii

After reviewing the whole area and considering over again the reconstruction work of the future, Mahatma Gandhi presided at a meeting of the All-India Committee of the Central Relief work, and moved the following resolution from the chair:

"This Committee tenders its respectful co-operation to Government in prosecution of the common object of relieving the unparalleled distress that has overtaken Bihar."

Although, he said, himself a confirmed non-co-operator, he had no doubt whatsoever that on this occasion they should offer their co-operation to Government, and if they did so it must, of course, be offered respectfully. He held this view, because he felt that in this crisis there was no other course but co-operation open before them. In view of the magnitude of the work they could not do without Government's assistance, just as Government could not do without theirs. The crisis was well calculated to bring them all together, and banish, for the time being, all differences, political and racial. According to non-official estimates twenty thousand, and according to official records many thousand people had lost their lives. All differences were hushed and old enmities forgotten on the cremation-ground.

They worked to-day not as Congressmen but as humanitarians. Throughout his recent tour he never had occasion even once to mention the name of Congress. They had but one object, and that was the service of the stricken people.

ix

In all that he thus spoke so movingly and generously, as the Chairman of the greatest gathering of Indian leaders ever held in connection with the Central Relief Fund, he was truly representing the best mind of India.

For there is a sincere longing for co-operation, if only it can be carried out on honourable and equal terms. No one feels this and understands it more than Gandhi himself. It is also the deepest sentiment with Tagore.

By far the most serious obstacle in the past, in the way of such honourable co-operation, has been the attitude of racial superiority which meets Indians at every turn, and is rightly resented by them.

No better opportunity could be offered for the abandonment of such an attitude, in face of human suffering, than the present situation affords. Not merely the earthquake relief problem, but the whole future of India in its relation to the Western Powers seems to depend on this one issue.

CHAPTER X

THE GREAT EXPERIMENT

i

IT is noticeable that everyone who has visited the stricken area in North Bihar has commented on the fact that in most of the larger towns, such as Monghyr and Muzaffarpur, the narrowness of the streets proved the main cause of the high death-rate.

The Bihar Government rightly called these narrow streets in the bazaars a "death trap." Among the recommendations for the future, the widening of all the streets in the new townships has taken a prominent place. Those whose lives were saved told the story, how the people ran in terror out of their houses only to see the walls on either side collapse. It was indeed a "death trap" without any means of escape!

ii

Not merely for safety's sake, but also for health and other reasons, it is obviously imperative that the new buildings shall be planned on a better model than the past. This can only be accomplished, with justice to all, and without base profiteering, if every part of the new town planning, including the rates charged for all material, is controlled by a central authority, acting on its own initiative, and having final powers of decision.

This central authority must obviously be the Relief

THE INDIAN EARTHQUAKE

Commissioner, Mr. Brett, with his expert technical staff, acting in different fields as his advisers and agents, carrying out his main purpose.

All this may be taken for granted, as things stand to-day in Bihar; and Government would have been rightly blamed if the initiative had not immediately been taken in town and village planning.

But in a country like India, where the National Movement has become a passion among all the finest minds in the younger generation, difficulties are certain to arise unless leading officials spend much time in carrying with them in their new proposals both the Indian leaders and also the younger people who are working with them.

They will be wise, therefore, to lay aside other things, however important, in order to explain, every step of the way, the value of what they propose to do. This must be done in a friendly and understanding manner, if it is to have any effect, and every touch of race superiority must vanish.

If, from the very beginning, time is carefully spent in establishing these friendly contacts, then the reconstruction and relief work will go smoothly. Personal difficulties will become reduced to a minimum, and cordial support will be given to every part of the new "planning" that is obviously best for the people. The volunteer workers will also be able to explain to the people themselves what is being undertaken, and thus gain their support and co-operation.

But if, on the contrary, careful attention is *not* given by those in authority to this personal factor; if attempts are made to ride roughshod over those who are devoting their whole service to the national cause, as they regard it, then even those improvements in "planning," which seem to be most suitable in the new townships, are likely at some point or other to be held up, or to break down, owing to a lack of personal understanding. Then, even if in the end the whole matter is pushed through by a Government order, a great deal of its value as a reconstructive measure will be lost.

Truisms such as these which I have been constantly repeating in this book may appear superfluous. But I have so often seen the disastrous collapse of co-operative effort and the bitterness on both sides that has resulted that I would wish at the outset to set down a warning based on painful practical experience.

iii

With whole-hearted co-operation guaranteed both by the whole body of national workers and also by those dwellers in North Bihar who have eagerly invited their assistance, I can place no limit to the improvement which may be brought about by drastic measures of reconstruction in the province. The hard crust of centuries of custom has been broken through by this earthquake shock, and society has become for the first time, after years of unbroken tradition, malleable and pliable to an extraordinary degree. Life can never be the same again. Therefore if the Great Experiment, as I would call it, of town and village planning can be carried through with

THE INDIAN EARTHQUAKE

the cordial co-operation and goodwill of all concerned, and on the best possible lines, it will be a noble achievement. Furthermore, it will not affect merely the north of the province of Bihar, but will afford an example to the whole of India of what such co-operation can affect.

iv

It would be abundantly worth while, in this special connection, for the Government of India to make a request to the Japanese Government, which would surely be granted, to allow a personal visit of inspection by chosen representatives from the earthquake area in India to the cities of Tokyo and Yokohama and the surrounding country, which were stricken more than ten years ago. It might be possible for these Indian visitors to obtain facilities, not only to see what had been accomplished by a sister nation, but also to learn how everything was done, and what difficulties had to be overcome.

Since the "planning" and reconstruction work in North Bihar is likely to cover a series of years and to be fraught with peculiar difficulties, such an enquiry would amply repay itself in the future. Large minds are surely needed to carry through big designs.

There is a celebrated passage in the life of Cecil Rhodes, in South Africa, where a new undertaking was to be attempted, and he was asked by his agents for his own instructions. Cecil Rhodes cabled back, "Consult Luke xiv. 28."

The text indicated that before starting to build a tower

THE GREAT EXPERIMENT

it was necessary to "sit down and count the cost." The very word "planning" implies this, and the proverb which Rhodes thus cited in South Africa is apt also for this Great Experiment in North Bihar.

V

It is surely a splendid asset that Rajendra Prasad, the Chairman of the Central Relief Committee, from the first moment when he grasped the situation, began to think in big terms about reconstruction, and was not content with small designs.

It was also equally valuable and timely that Mahatma Gandhi, after seeing the appalling extent of the disaster, declared in outspoken terms, which reached the whole of India, that Co-operation must be the watchword for the future, and that by a united effort between the Government and the people this calamity must be turned from a curse into a blessing. He went further and pressed this need of united action on all classes of the community.

"I wish everyone," he declared, "without distinction of race, religion, and creed, including Government servants, to give all the help they can to the sufferers in Bihar."

He went on to warn, with a tender yet stern affection, each villager who might be in need of relief to *work* for it and not to seek it as a beggar. True self-respect, he urged, must be maintained by each individual, and manual labour must be given to the fullest extent possible in return for money: only the maimed and the injured, who were quite unable to work, should consent to receive alms.

vi

Turning aside from the towns and the literate population to the semi-illiterate village people, who number over twelve millions in the scattered villages of North Bihar, there is only one power which can make a direct universal appeal—Religion. Whenever it is imperative to speak to the heart and conscience of the 90 per cent in India who live in the villages, the religious motive is far stronger than the economic. For the religious motive may bring about a change from within which no outward incentive can accomplish.

Religion is still supreme in India to a degree that is hard to understand in the West. The only parallel is that of Europe in the Middle Ages, when a St. Bernard or a St. Francis could carry through changes which could never have been brought about by any other power on earth.

Thus to-day, when it is necessary above all things, while rebuilding, to get rid of recognized abuses, such as early child-marriage and the curse of untouchability, which destroy all healthy village life and defeat all hope of social progress, only a prophet who has been raised up to do the work, like Mahatma Gandhi, can effect this permanent inward change. However necessary legislation may be, it is ineffective until the heart has been touched and the conscience accepts the religious sanction.

I have before me a document written by one of the

THE GREAT EXPERIMENT

keenest minds in South India, a lawyer who has given up his practice for the national cause. He has pondered deeply over what he has seen recently in Madras, where the curse of untouchability is most deep-seated, and he has sent me a copy of what he had written. Though a Hindu, he has begun with a quotation from the Gospel:

"And there gathered unto Jesus a great multitude, so that He entered into a ship and sat on the sea: and the whole multitude was by the sea on the land."

"Mahatma Gandhi's tour," he writes, "which has just been finished in the South, must be classed among the most remarkable psychological phenomena of all time. Something like it is seen in the pages of the Bible, wherefrom the above passage is taken. *If I had not seen it all with my own eyes, I would have sworn it could not be.*"

The writer then goes on to describe what he has seen, —the hundreds of thousands of villagers, who have waited patiently, hour after hour, to see Gandhi.

"What," he asks, "is the secret of this strange attachment? Gandhi declares himself a destroyer of what these people regard as a part of their sacred Hindu religion —the maintenance of the 'untouchable' barrier. And yet they hail him as a prophet and crowd literally in their thousands to get a sight of him."

The writer then gives the only answer which fits the facts. They regard, he says, Mahatma Gandhi as a man of God. Therefore they are ready to give up even these age-long traditions, based on ignorance and superstition, in response to his call. No other power on earth can break that tradition, except the word of a prophet of God.

vii

What does this mean in North Bihar? We do not want to build up over again those wretched filth-laden villages, where "touchable" and "untouchable" are obliged to live apart, and children are born in thousands only to die in infancy. God forbid! The human asset—the gentleness, goodness, and patience of the people—is so excellent. Everyone who lives among them loves them. But the ignorance, the miserable insanitation, and almost childish superstition are so vast. How is it possible to enlighten them about the most obvious things and yet keep intact their splendidly simple character?

Only a prophet can do this, and Mahatma Gandhi, by his life and work among them, has already shown the way. He is a born "villager." He speaks to them in their own accent—"in their own tongue, wherein they were born." They count him as their own: he is one of themselves.

We may spend all our years to find that way to speak to them, and fail. He is born with this quality, and bred with it also from his mother's knee. He will live with it and die with it; and all the years he spent in London and South Africa have never changed him.

Gandhi is right, in one sense, about the earthquake itself. The Law of Gravitation, impersonal as Fate, was the cause of it—he acknowledges this. But there was a

THE GREAT EXPERIMENT

moral earthquake which came with it, upheaving those villagers' minds. It shook them, for the moment, from age-long custom, which lay upon them—

> with a weight,
> Heavy as frost, and deep almost as life.

That Muslim on the bank of the Ganges who saw the river vanish cried *Quyāmat!*—"The Day of Judgment!"[1] That was what the villagers all thought.

A prophet can surely use this great occasion and shake these village people's hearts towards repentance and amendment: he can make clear to them, in his own way, the meaning of the moral shock they have received. He can bring it home to their hearts and consciences.— Can we?

Kagawa in Japan was able to shake the conscience of his own nation after the earthquake of 1923. He spoke and wrote then as a prophet in their own tongue. His pamphlets reached a circulation of two million copies. Gandhi can do the same thing in India. That is his great power!

Let us go back again to the keenly observant mind of the Hindu writer in Madras, from whom I have already quoted:

"It is silly," he writes, with a note of impatience at the folly of it, "for Government to try to bring about changes in India without getting the co-operation of Gandhi. The folly is all the greater when it is admitted that he is eager and ready to co-operate. . . . What a

[1] See p. 20.

THE INDIAN EARTHQUAKE

tragedy that these forces of human progress should remain unutilized!"

"What a tragedy!" That is surely what every man and woman of goodwill is likely to say in face of human suffering so great.

viii

The watchful intelligence of Tagore will also be needed. Gandhi himself has recognized this; and he values Tagore's judgment, even when it goes against him. He has called Tagore, in these moral issues, "The Great Sentinel." He has clung to his support and companionship through all the strange vicissitudes of his career. For when the fire burns within, the passionate utterance of the man of God may often carry him beyond bounds. Gandhi himself has humbly realized this weakness.

But no one living has Gandhi's volcanic power—his stark, naked truthfulness—the consuming fire within—that "Woe is me, if I preach not," which consumed St. Paul. And when the question arises, not of mending here and patching there, but of bringing about a change of heart, then the unique value of one who can drive the message home among millions of men should be realized by everyone who is a true statesman in human affairs.

CHAPTER XI

THE SPIRIT OF SERVICE

i

THIS chapter is written chiefly for those who have not lived in India for any long period, and therefore have had no personal experience of that joy in the spirit of service which is to be found so abundantly in that country, especially in the new generation.

The contact with the West resulted at first in a great historical change, starting from Bengal, which is called the Indian Renaissance. It began under the inspiring leadership of one of the noblest men of his or any other age, Raja Ram Mohan Roy. The movement carried within it an intense love of freedom and self-expression.

That Renaissance spirit is still active to-day. It has had its saints and martyrs, its scholars and poets, who have made the greatest sacrifices to bring to an end some evil custom or out-worn tradition. Each part of India in turn has experienced its moving power.

There is an Indian word, commonly used in most of the Indian languages, whose root meaning is Service (Seva). In a remarkable way it has continually enlarged its currency in recent years both in political and social relations. It implies that the greatest of all reforms may be wrought by those who serve their fellow-men rather than by those who rule. In this respect it is in keeping with a memorable passage in the Gospels where Christ says to His disciples, "The Kings of the Gentiles exercise lordship . . . but it shall not be so with you. . . . For I am among you as He that serveth."[1]

The genius of Mr. G. K. Gokhale made noble use of this conception. He called his political institution "The Servants of India Society." With its abbreviated title, "Servindia," it has kept true to the spirit of its founder. We have again the "Seva Sadan," representing woman's work of service; and again the "Servants of the People," started by Lala Lajpat Rai; and last of all, "The Servants of the Untouchables," of which G. D. Birla is President, and A. V. Thakkar Organizing Secretary.

ii

Owing to Swami Vivekananda, the word "Seva" has also come back into use in its religious sense of worship—the service of God. He made the service of the poor a part of all true worship. In such worship (or service) there could be no patronage but only devotion. For God was there before us in the poor man; and the one who served the poor worshipped God. The Sevasrams of the Ramkrishna Mission, founded by Vivekananda, carry on his noble work. In every disaster of flood or famine in India, as I have personally witnessed, the monks of this Mission are among the first to render service.

In the North of India, Swami Dayananda Saraswati broke up much of the hard ground in the field of social

[1] Luke xxii. 24-28.

THE SPIRIT OF SERVICE

and domestic reform. The Gurukulas,[1] founded in his name, send out their social workers in times of emergency. Ever since his day the Arya Samaj, which he instituted to carry on his work, has led the van in many forms of social activity.

Among the Muslims also reforming movements have spread. Sir Syed Ahmed, in his own great way, at Aligarh broke through the hard crust of convention, and thus led to a notable advance in Islam.

All through the nineteenth century, especially in the South, Christian Missions have had their own great part to play. Hospitals, leper-houses, have sprung up, revealing Christ's love for the poor. The Christa Seva Sangha at Poona ("Christ Service Society") shows the natural adaptation of the word "Seva" in a Christian setting.

iii

All these varied and distinct efforts, which had run their course before the World War and had achieved noble results, have now been caught up in the one sweeping tide of the National Movement, which has passed not merely over India but the whole of Asia. Hindu, Muslim, Sikh, Parsee, Christian—all alike have felt its rapid current carrying them along. The spirit of sacrifice and service, which had appeared in individuals before, has now been shown with remarkable power among the masses of the people. Whenever the summons has come to face some national crisis or danger, men and women have stepped fearlessly forward.

[1] Schools under the moral discipline of a Guru.

THE INDIAN EARTHQUAKE

One of the most salutary changes which the National Movement has brought with it has been to direct the attention of Young India away from the towns to the villages. For it cannot be too clearly understood that nine out of ten of the countless millions of India live in villages. India is a country of villages.

Those who are educated to-day in Gurukulas, or in different Asrams; or have joined some Youth Movement; or belong to some organ of social service, no longer hold aloof from the hard life of village poverty, where town comforts are not available, but work in the villages carrying out there an intensive reform programme. This always includes, as its chief duty, the removal of the ban of untouchability—the curse of being treated as a pariah—which still hangs over the heads of no less than forty-five million human beings.

It is true that the end of this national effort is Swaraj—a political goal. But the leaders of Young India recognize with open eyes that no Swaraj worthy of the name can ever be realized unless practical social problems such as these, which strike at the root of village life and destroy unity, are boldly tackled and solved.

iv

All this brings us directly to the earthquake disaster in North Bihar. For India, like China, is a country where the giant forces of Nature on rare occasions run riot, bringing ruin and misery to millions of village people.

The embankments of some great river will suddenly

THE SPIRIT OF SERVICE

give way and the waters will sweep over the country; a flood, during the monsoon, will destroy all the standing crops; a famine scarcity will arise through a drought in the rainy season; a cholera epidemic will break out in the villages, which must at once be brought under control, if thousands of lives are to be saved.

The villagers themselves, in face of such overwhelming calamities, however brave and long-suffering they may be, are often helpless. They live from hand to mouth, and have nothing to fall back on if the crops fail. But Young China and Young India have both learnt with extraordinary promptness to come to the rescue of the poor, and a band of volunteers is always available for this purpose.

V

In order to make this general description more concrete, let me take from my own experience an example of active service in a flooded area of North Bengal some years ago. All the conditions were similar to those which I have seen this year in the earthquake area after the monsoon. The whole countryside was inundated for nearly two thousand square miles, and the villagers were the chief sufferers.

On that previous occasion national volunteers came forward from every part of India. It was noticeable that while the flooded area was predominantly Muslim, the greater proportion of relief workers were Hindu students. All religious barriers were broken down. Only those who were entirely fearless could join in the work, for there was much danger from epidemic disease connected with it.

THE INDIAN EARTHQUAKE

Remote villages had to be reached in boats where people were on the verge of starvation. At other places the mud was many inches deep. Fever was prevalent, and cholera was always at the door. The sick and dying had to be tended increasingly.

The area in which our own party was working covered sixty square miles. The inundated area was one vast plain intersected by many rivers which had overflowed their banks.

Every worker was a volunteer, living in a camp in the simplest manner possible. Most of them were under twenty years of age. Those who took the lead and did the best work were certainly those who had come from different Asrams. There were also students from the colleges, who had obtained leave of absence and worked with us in a very noble manner.

These national volunteers had a perfect genius for this form of social service, and accepted its hard discipline without a murmur. Indeed, they thoroughly enjoyed it, so that the whole camp rang with their singing when they came back in the evening. They had also learnt to perform with their own hands the most menial tasks, such as formerly had been left to "sweepers." They took actual pleasure in breaking through old inhibitions and doing these things personally.

vi

Looking back on my own past experience of India, I cannot imagine all this work having been done by the

THE SPIRIT OF SERVICE

young, in such a gay and gallant manner, thirty years ago. The kindly instinct was there, but it had not been evoked; and there were strict religious taboos blocking the way. There was also a tendency to leave everything to the officials.

But in these recent years—such has been my constant experience—wherever the call has come and a great national leader has given the word, the response has been spontaneous. Death itself has often had to be faced in volunteering for such service. Not seldom, health has been so sorely impaired that the marks of the hardship have remained for many years. But this does not daunt in the least those who offer and obey the call. Indeed, in a cholera camp, and in other circumstances also, the greatest difficulty of all has been to get those who are young and brave to take sufficient personal precaution when dealing with disease.

Perhaps the most significant thing of all during recent years has been the way in which the women of India have come forward to take their part side by side with the men. This was very noticeable when meeting the distress caused by the floods in Orissa; and I have been informed that the same characteristic has been marked again more recently in North Bihar.

There is a wealth of sacrifice and devotion stored up in the hearts of the women of India which will one day prove an incalculable treasure for the country at large. Now at last that day seems to have dawned, and this great fund of loving service has begun to find its way into a wider circulation far beyond the narrow confines of the home. Every kind of generous social work will be enriched thereby.

vii

The desire of Young India to answer the call of sacrifice and service, when it comes, with a chivalrous appeal to help the weak, will at once awaken a response in the hearts of the young in the West. For nothing draws the youth of the world closer together than high endeavour of this kind. It comes with a human touch, and humanity everywhere is moved by it.

Therefore, in this great affliction, which has singled out India among the nations as the sufferer, the West will surely be ready to take its own share of relief work, if only the right way can be pointed out whereby this may best be accomplished.

CHAPTER XII

THE MONSOON FLOODS

i

LONG before the normal monsoon rains had made their appearance in northern India careful preparations had been made by the Central Relief Committee to forestall disaster in the earthquake-stricken area. The contour survey, made by the Government surveyors, showed that less displacement of masses of land on a huge scale had occurred than had originally been estimated. But only the monsoon rains themselves could show what would be the final effect of the changes made by the earthquake in the land surface of North Bihar.

Meanwhile, during the months of March, April, and May, several flotillas of flat-bottomed boats and rafts were constructed and stationed at all the danger-points. Here the Government officials and the national volunteers worked splendidly together, according to a prepared plan, so that nothing was left to chance when the heavy rains came.

The towns, which had been ruined by the earthquake, were for the most part left unbuilt, until the monsoon should show clearly how the water would lie on ground after the floods had subsided and what sites would be high above flood-level.

When I reached India in August the monsoon rains were in excess along the northern plain of which Bihar forms an integral part. The north-east corner had suffered severely from floods after the first outburst of the monsoon, and immense damage had been done. Both the upper and lower valleys of Assam had been flooded out. Villages had been swept away and lives had been lost.

The River Brahmaputra had so completely overflowed its banks that its main stream was many miles across. Thousands of square miles had been deluged. The villages along its banks were completely cut off for many days, and the distress was extreme.

ii

These abnormally heavy monsoon rains travelled along the foot-hills of the Himalayas until they reached North Bihar. Here also the rainfall was excessive. An increasing downpour continued day and night. The rivers in the earthquake-stricken area soon became quite incapable of carrying off the flood-waters into the River Ganges. Lakes and lagoons were formed, which did not empty themselves into the river courses but remained stagnant week after week without subsiding.

As had been already feared, very large areas of the upper part of North Bihar thus became water-logged. The paddy, which had been sown, perished. The villagers themselves were rescued in boats, and their cattle also were saved in the same manner; but any hope of a harvest from the soil had to be abandoned. The men and women were given work to do in order to keep them from starvation.

THE MONSOON FLOODS

The greatness of this excess of rainfall on the north-eastern side of India may be statistically realized when it is told that Cherrapunji—the spur standing out above the plain where the monsoon first strikes the mountains —received over 118 inches of rain in a single week, thus beating its own previous record!

Meanwhile the Arabian Sea monsoon current had also been active. It struck the hills in the extreme north-west of India and produced quite unusual floods in that region. As it passed down the great mountain barrier towards the centre of the Himalayas it filled all the rivers. Both the Jumna and the Ganges, which rise in the deep recesses of the mountains, began to send down an excess of rain-water, which made them overflow.

Furthermore, the hills in the centre of India, to the south of the River Ganges, also received an abnormal share of the monsoon rains this year, and the tributaries which flow into the River Ganges from the south rose at the same time up to flood-level.

Just above Patna there is a confluence of waters where different rivers meet to join the main stream of the Ganges. The heavy rainfall of the monsoon now began to cause a congestion or overflow at this meeting-point, and a vast new flood occurred which threatened Patna itself. The lower portion of the North Bihar plain suffered most of all. Certain portions which had been inundated by the first flood were again flooded out by the second rising of the waters.

As if this was not sufficient, a third flood came later on, and it seemed as if human endurance had at last reached its breaking-point. The waters of the Jumna and the Ganges which had been already swollen higher upstream now rose to an excessive height at their junction at Allahabad and came pouring down in a full flood-tide past Benares until they reached the danger-point at Patna. Here they covered again a large portion of the plain of North Bihar with their overflow and threatened another vast inundation.

iii

It was at this time that a tragedy occurred whereby a young national volunteer lost his life. The difficulties of crossing over to the northern side of the River Ganges, when it is in full flood, are very great. Steamers cease to ply backward and forward. Country boats are used when making the risky journey. One of these was taking across a band of relief workers when it was upset in the whirling current. The rest of the volunteers were rescued many miles downstream. But it was found that one of their number was missing.

A lad was taken out of the water unconscious, opposite Monghyr—more than thirty miles downstream—and at first it was hoped that this might be the missing relief worker. But it proved to be someone else, and no further news has been heard of the young volunteer who thus sacrificed his life for those he came to help. Before he thus gave his own life for others he had saved the lives of many villagers by his fearless rescue work during the height of the floods.

THE MONSOON FLOODS

iv

The question may be asked whether the heavy rains this year have done good as well as harm. The answer is now fairly certain, that some good results have followed. The layers of sand, for instance, which had caused such injury to the alluvial soil, have in places been washed clean away. In other parts they have been considerably lightened. Thus the "sand" problem does not look so formidable to-day as it did before the monsoon.

Again the tributary rivers, which flow from the hills into the ganges, have had their river-beds scoured by the excess of rainfall. Nature has done her own recuperative work. Though this excessive rain has destroyed the crops, and ruined also a large number of villages in the flooded area, it has undoubtedly helped to fill in the gaping cracks in the earth's surface caused by the earthquake, while in other places it has converted these fissures themselves into new water-courses.

Yet the damage done has been enormous. In one of the districts of North Bihar, which was stricken by the earthquake, a relief worker told me that the inhabitants, without exception, declared that the damage done and the suffering caused by the recent floods had been greater than that from which they had suffered in the earthquake itself. It will be extremely hard for the long-enduring villagers to sustain courage and hope for another year. The need for the enthusiasm and active support of the national volunteers will be greater than ever before.

On enquiry it was found that the Viceroy's Fund could

THE INDIAN EARTHQUAKE

not cover the damage done by the floods in North Bihar. It has therefore been thought advisable to close down this Fund altogether, along with the Lord Mayor of London's Fund which assisted it.

The People's Fund, administered by the Central Relief Committee, is under no such restriction, and may be used for the relief of those who have suffered from the floods in the earthquake area. Its need of continued support will be greater than ever before.

V

The work of the volunteers in rescuing the villagers and the cattle marooned by floods such as these is peculiarly difficult.

Hundreds of square miles are covered with water over which the relief boats must ply as they go from village to village. The villages are like islands, crowded with human beings and with cattle. Even at the end of September I could see stretches of water as far as the eye could reach, like one vast shallow sea, with here and there a clump of trees that denoted human habitations.

Sometimes, just as the waters begin to subside, the deluge of rain starts over again. The rivers become swollen once more, and the waters rise till even the mounds where the peasants and their cattle have sought refuge are submerged.

Then, later on, at the beginning of the cold weather after the rains, when the floods have subsided, the ground is thick with mud, from which rank mists rise as night comes on. A raw wind also blows down from the hills at dawn. Disease seizes its victims who have no staying power of resistance.

Again and again I have witnessed such scenes, and I have wondered how human endurance could stand the strain.

CHAPTER XIII

INTERNATIONAL HELP

i

WHEN the distress in India, caused by the earthquake, seemed to have reached its highest point, and the human need for sympathy was most poignant, I received a letter from Dr. Pierre Cérésole in Switzerland suggesting that if the call were very urgent he could make himself free to go out at once to India in order to see for himself what had happened, and give help where he could. He then might come back to Europe, if the need itself called for such action, and bring with him to India in the cold weather an international team to help side by side with the Indian workers in the larger work of reconstruction and relief.

Dr. Cérésole had already met me in England, in years gone by, and I had heard much about the work which his organization—the International Volunteer Service—had accomplished in Europe.

During the World War he had felt, as a civil engineer with practical experience, that if he could organize a body of young men to do the most difficult constructive work, at times of natural disaster—such as a flood or an avalanche—this work might afford full and noble expression for that courageous hardship which formed, for young men, one of the great attractions of war. He therefore organized a "peace service" of this heroic

INTERNATIONAL HELP

kind as a counterpart to "war service." The peace service would be constructive, while the war service was clearly destructive.

He worked along with his voluntary team, using hard manual labour, in restoring devastated or derelict areas. At Liechtenstein in Germany, where a river-dam had burst; in Switzerland, where an avalanche had destroyed two villages; in South Wales, at Brynmawr, where a derelict area had been left after the mines had closed down—in all these places he had already done reconstructive work, which had gained for his movement an international reputation. All over the Continent of Europe his name is well known and respected.

ii

It seemed to me, therefore, that here might be the very answer to the request which had been so often made to me from India, that I should seek for European aid. Even if, in the acute economic depression, large sums of money could not easily be sent out, here was something far more valuable than money, namely, sympathy expressed in personal service. Therefore on receiving Dr. Cérésole's letter I went out to Gland, in Switzerland, where we met together; and it was quickly decided between us that he should go out by the next available steamer, which started from Venice on April 13.

He arrived in Bombay on April 26, 1934, and was most cordially received. Then he went on immediately to the distressed area in company with Rajendra Prasad.

THE INDIAN EARTHQUAKE

Since that date I have received a cable from him stating that all had gone well, and that he was already proposing, if funds allowed, to bring out international workers in the cold weather.

Rajendra Prasad also sent me a long message, telling me with what joy the arrival of Dr. Cérésole had been welcomed in India, and what an encouragement it had been to have his presence with them. His coming out had made a deep impression, and had shown in a practical manner the sympathy of the West.[1]

iii

Though it is still premature, it may be well to record one practical suggestion that I have made. If from any one country representatives are selected to go out, the country to which they belong might be asked to provide by public subscription their travelling expenses. This would at once relieve Dr. Cérésole of much of the financial difficulty connected with the scheme, and would also not impose too heavy a burden on any one country.

iv

While visiting during the past months the different capitals of Europe in order to make known the extent of the earthquake disaster in India, I was deeply interested to find among the younger members of each nation a true sympathy and understanding.

[1] Dr. Pierre Cérésole met me at Marseilles on October 19th, and we had a long consultation together about the future. His letter to me will be found in the Appendix, page 123.

INTERNATIONAL HELP

For instance, when I was asked to broadcast about the Indian earthquake from Copenhagen, a correspondence followed in which earnest questions were asked about personal service. One young man who came to see me was eager to go out if an international team was formed and his own duties allowed him to go. Other requests of a similar character were made in different places, so that I have confidence that if the need were strongly expressed in India by Indian leaders, the sympathy of Europe would at once take this practical turn. In my own country, England, it seems to me certain that a ready response would be given.

The fact that things have gone so far, and that the wish to help has already been expressed from so many quarters, should give cheer and encouragement in India, where I have already made it known. There also, in the economic depression, money is hard to get in large amounts, but personal service is highly valued. The Indian leaders, therefore, will take count of a world phenomenon, and not be disappointed at the smallness of financial aid, where the much higher form of sympathy in personal ways is made evident.

Those also should surely be encouraged who are eagerly seeking for avenues whereby the whole world may be drawn closer together on the basis of equal friendship and service.

v

With such tentative conclusions as these, and with many misgivings because of the circumstances in which this

THE INDIAN EARTHQUAKE

volume has been written, I would venture to launch it forth. The difficulties of incessant travel and the absence from books of reference have obviously made it very far from being the book I wished to write. But during my journeys to and fro, both in my own country and in the rest of Europe, I was continually faced with the fact that the whole picture had not yet been given in the West in a form which could easily be understood. For that reason the attempt has been made.

I can see a great danger ahead, that East and West—each concerned with its own immediate interests—may drift further and further apart. There are also bitternesses hard to control. This very calamity of the great earthquake in Bihar seemed to present to me a human standpoint, where everything else might be left on one side and only our common humanity might be brought forward. In that faith and hope this volume has been written.

APPENDIX

A LETTER FROM PIERRE CÉRÉSOLE

WHILE you are away in South Africa, our friends in London suggest that, with your consent, I might add a few lines to your book. It sounds almost like an impertinence. Nevertheless I gladly accept the suggestion. If I do so in the form of a letter written to you, I shall feel all the time that I am addressing the most friendly and benevolent British reader, and there will be no inhibition and no difficulties.

Do you remember Sibford, where we met for the first time? It was exactly the right place to meet you—so truly English. We both spoke at the Conference of the Fellowship of Reconciliation, and I was much impressed by what you told us on the religious attitude of the people in India. You couldn't be equally struck by what I said about "International Voluntary Service for Peace," because you didn't attend my lecture. You were right. All I have to say and to repeat goes in very few words: "Let us harness for peace all the splendid forces so far wasted in war and war preparation." It is no use talking much about it—our real business is to go and do it.

Volunteers from all parts of Europe and of America have now been at this voluntary peace service for nearly fifteen years—since the end of the war—doing their best to repair the effects of various catastrophes—avalanche, landslide, flood, unemployment—in France, Switzerland,

THE INDIAN EARTHQUAKE

Liechtenstein, Great Britain. This year again we had four services—two in England and two in Switzerland. More than two thousand men and women so far have taken part in the work organized by our international voluntary service.

But our common "concern"—for you and for me—appeared only with the earthquake of January 15, 1934, in India. After an extremely short parley, the way seeming as clear as it could be, you sent me to India. I stayed there seven weeks, minus one day. What is to be seen in the devastated area is perfectly described in your own pages.

And we ask now: "Is it reasonable to offer the help of the International Voluntary Service for Peace in Bihar?"

The answer would be "Emphatically no" if it were a question of material reparation only. We had much better, in that case, send all the money we may dispose of to other excellent relief organizations already at work. But there is another side to this matter.

When Mathura Prasad—my devoted guide—took me out to the peasants of Patahi, for instance, they were rather puzzled at first: "What is this new tall European wanting here?" We assembled under a big tree and—Mathura translating from English into Hindi—I explained my point.

I spoke about the war: how it had been in terms of lives, crops, villages, and towns destroyed—a thousand times worse than their earthquake; how it had wiped out in certain cases, not only a village, but the very place

A LETTER FROM PIERRE CÉRÉSOLE

where the village had stood: e.g. the hill of Vaugois. "What we want now is something to prevent *that* from recurring." And I described the spirit which makes for war: every man and every nation caring first for oneself; and the spirit which makes for peace: every man and every nation caring first for the good of the community. "This spirit of peace service, if we could get it, would at one and the same time make war impossible, and supply instantly all means necessary to repair the effects of the worst natural catastrophe. Nobody has any reason to "complain against God" about natural catastrophies so long as free human ingenuity is applied to organize still greater ones. And finally, "Our International Voluntary Service would like to help you, not only with money, but also, as far as possible, by the living, personal collaboration of some of our men; this being, in our opinion, the best way to raise and strengthen the new spirit without which humanity seems doomed to death."

So the peasants of Patahi and many other villages which we visited understood well what I meant by the "other side" of our action, beyond and above material help. Our coming will be understood and welcomed by them. But it would be quite wrong to suppose that its moral effect will be felt only, or even mainly, in the villages receiving direct benefit. The work we organized between 1920 and 1921 in Esnes, near Verdun, for instance, may have left very little trace among the local people, but it was and remains an inspiration and an incentive for many hundreds who heard about it all over the world.

THE INDIAN EARTHQUAKE

Our aim is reached wherever somebody, hearing of our effort, gets a clearer vision of what might happen if the millions of young men preparing to-day for mutual destruction could be turned to construction with all the wealth, material, intellectual and spiritual, involved and invested at present in military institutions. In a few weeks the peace army would easily clear, reclaim, or rebuild everything which needs clearing, reclaiming, or rebuilding in Bihar.

A miracle of this kind, or even the smaller one we might have in view now, should not be allowed to take place, in the present circumstances, in India without definite precautions. Volunteers—even working without wages and receiving only their normal, plain food—might seem a small comfort to an Indian peasant if this peasant were half-starving and only too glad to do the reparation work himself at a fraction of the cost represented by the foreigner's food alone. We have therefore to reduce to an absolute minimum the costs involved by non-Indian help without cutting out altogether our personal co-operation.

What I propose, starting on the smallest scale, is this. I would go back to India in October with the return of the cool and dry season, taking with me the funds necessary to pay for the food of fifty peasants for six months, something like £300, including my own travelling expenses. These peasants, with volunteers drawn if possible from other sections of the Indian people, together with myself and a good interpreter, would make the first "Unit" to be placed under the direction of the

A LETTER FROM PIERRE CÉRÉSOLE

Bihar Central Relief Committee and of its President, Rajendra Prasad.

As a "delegate" of the I.V.S., my part would be to work as much as possible with the other members of the unit in the field. The delegate is not meant to give "superior advice." Placed under the Relief Committee, we shall ask Rajendra Prasad to choose some competent Indian leader of the unit for the best progress of the work.

This describes one unit. Any number of similar units might be formed according to our resources and money, and in men competent to fulfil the somewhat delicate functions of the I.V.S. delegate. I hope that, according to your suggestions, several countries will themselves find both the men and the money necessary for their own unit.

The amount of money to be spent on travelling expenses for the single volunteer to India remains large in comparison with what is needed for the fifty Indian members of the Unit. But if international goodwill has the value we claim for it, this expenditure is justified. It remains infinitesimal in regard to the tremendous sums spent during the war to carry many hundred thousands of men over a quarter, or half, the trip around the world—many thousands of them coming from India —to the battlefields of France, or of the Dardenelles, for slaughter and destruction. To prevent this happening again we may well, as a beginning, bring half a dozen peace workers for reconstruction in India.

The plan suggested is quite practical, and has met

THE INDIAN EARTHQUAKE

with the approval of the National Relief workers and of the Government officials.

It has been of the greatest importance that you, Charlie, together with the most active friends of India in Great Britain, should have been the main instruments in setting our I.V.S. in motion for the relief work in Bihar. This clears automatically many misunderstandings. It was my privilege and particular satisfaction to repeat at every turn in India that I had been sent by you and by the best friends India has in the world.

I explained also that, while visiting or working under the immediate direction of the National Relief Committee, we had not in mind to meddle with thorny political problems which did not concern us, but to support whole-heartedly the spirit of non-violence—*Ahimsa*—on which the future of the human race seems to depend. We shall do everything in our power to promote constructive collaboration between all men of goodwill, whatever their political or religious creed.

No funds shall be used for this scheme except those *specially* given for the purpose by people interested in the work of international and inter-racial reconciliation connected with this plan.

The opinion of the Indian friends on our plans is clearly expressed in a letter of Rajendra Prasad's:

"I attach much greater value to your endeavour than can be calculated in pounds and shillings, or acres of land cleared or numbers of houses reconstructed. . . . Your contact with our people will be helpful in establishing that mutual goodwill and fellow-feeling which are

A LETTER FROM PIERRE CÉRÉSOLE

necessary in a world teeming with all kinds of conflicts. I am therefore thankful that this calamity of ours may in its own humble way help towards a truer understanding between the West and the East."

The ideal delegate in India should be, in my opinion, practical, adaptable, and young, not only in hopes and thoughts, but in body—three points on which I may have legitimate doubts concerning my own qualifications for the job. I received, however, a remarkable encouragement.

Mahatma Gandhi constantly repeats that he wants freedom for India, not that she might isolate herself, but in order to put her free spirit in the service of all nations. It is exactly—transferred in the international world—the word of my countryman, Alexandre Visset, "I want a man to be free that he may become the servant of all."

Considering the tremendous importance of this issue for the whole world, who would not gladly face plague or cholera, if he could thus induce the British side to a more daring generosity, and the Indian to more unflinching patience still?

My own Swiss canton, Vaud, has been governed for two centuries and a half by a canton of another race, Berne. Conditions were in some regards similar to those realized between India and Great Britain. Now we are equal members of a happy Confederation. No violent revolution of the Vaudois has taken place, not a drop of Bernese blood was shed by our people. It is true that the armies of the French Revolution had to defeat the old Bernese regime before the change occurred. History,

THE INDIAN EARTHQUAKE

for a large-scale transposition to the circumstances of Great Britain and India, does not need to repeat itself, but might well improve. There is no necessity, if the same happy ending is to be reached, that Great Britain should be defeated by anyone, whether by Japanese, German, or Bolshevist. It would be sufficient that her best people should bring the majority to share their views.

Anything we could do in India to bring help in this direction, however small materially, would be immensely worth while.

Thanks for your call, dear friend. May we receive the strength necessary for His work.